Comptroller of the Currency
Administrator of National Banks

Credit Card Lending

Comptroller's Handbook

Narrative - October 1996, Procedures - March 1998

A

Assets

Background

The credit card has evolved over the last thirty years into one of the most accepted, convenient, and profitable financial products. It is accepted by millions of consumers and merchants worldwide as a routine means of payment for all varieties of products and services. The rapid growth of the credit card industry evidences the card's value to the financial community, including consumers, merchants, and issuing banks.

Credit cards play a role in the strategic plans of many banks C either as a card issuer, merchant acquirer, or an agent bank. Issuing banks are directly involved in the credit card business through the actual issuance of cards as a member of an interchange system. Issuing banks also hold or sell the credit card loans and, therefore, bear some credit risk. A merchant or acquiring bank is an entity that has entered into an agreement with a merchant to accept deposits generated by credit card transactions. Processing merchant sales drafts may result in customer charge backs and, therefore, result in some transaction risk to the merchant bank. An agent bank is a bank that has entered into an agreement to participate in another bank's card program, usually by turning over its applicants for credit cards to the bank administering the program and by acting as a depository for merchants.

This booklet discusses the operations of issuing banks. It provides guidance for examiners and banks regarding the types of elements usually found in systems maintained by prudent bankers. Specific items identified for inclusion in bank policies, procedures, and guidelines are not presented as a required checklist. Each bank and its systems will vary. Examiners and bankers should consider the circumstances of the individual bank to determine what system elements are essential.

The dynamics of today's credit card market make it necessary for the successful issuing bank to manage every aspect of the lending process. In the past, success may have just happened, but with today's strong competition from other issuers, including nonbanks, and rapidly changing technologies, every step in the lending function is crucial to maximizing profits. This booklet discusses each segment of an issuing bank's credit card operation, from marketing and account acquisition to collections. Each section has information on the necessary front- and back-end planning, controls, and monitoring necessary for success. (See the following chart titled "Credit Card Lending Process.")

Competition, market saturation, and changing consumer demographics and attitudes have also forced the successful issuing bank to be innovative with the credit card products it offers and its customer selection and management methods. This booklet discusses various types of credit card programs, such as affinity and cobranded cards, and the unique characteristics, risk, and controls necessary for each. This booklet also includes a discussion of credit scoring, since many issuing banks use this technology to help them identify possible customers and then manage the card holder accounts.

The rapid growth of credit cards also has caused banks to look elsewhere for funding rather than from traditional deposit accounts. This booklet briefly discusses the practice of securitizing credit card receivables as a funding vehicle for issuing banks.

As mentioned, a variety of factors have caused the credit card business to become one of the most complex and competitive areas in the financial services industry. The market environment and risks make it essential for issuing banks to have written operating policies tied to well-conceived business plans and risk management systems.

Risks Associated with Credit Card Lending

For purposes of the OCC's discussion of risk, examiners assess banking risk relative to its impact on capital and earnings. From a supervisory perspective, risk is the potential that events, expected or unanticipated, may have an adverse impact on the bank's capital or earnings. The OCC has defined nine categories of risk for bank supervision purposes. These risks are **Credit, Interest Rate, Liquidity, Price, Foreign Exchange, Transaction, Compliance, Strategic, and Reputation**. These categories are not mutually exclusive, any product or service may expose the bank to multiple risks. For analysis and discussion purposes, however, the OCC identifies and assesses the risks separately.

The primary risks associated with credit card lending are: **credit, transaction, liquidity, strategic, reputation, interest rate, and compliance risk.** These are discussed more fully in the following paragraphs.

Credit Risk

Credit risk is the risk to earnings or capital of an obligor's failure to meet the terms of any contract with the bank or otherwise fail to perform as agreed. Credit risk is found in all activities where success depends on counterparty, issuer, or borrower performance. It arises any time bank funds are extended, committed, invested or otherwise exposed through actual or implied contractual agreements, whether reflected on or off the balance sheet.

Credit risk poses the most significant risk to banks involved in credit card lending. Since credit card debt is an unsecured line of credit, repayment depends primarily upon a borrower's capacity to repay. The highly competitive environment for credit card lending has provided consumers with ample opportunity to hold several credit cards from different issuers and to pay only minimum monthly payments on outstanding balances. As a result, borrowers may become overextended and unable to repay, particularly in times of an economic downturn or a personal catastrophic event.

The majority of credit card programs are priced at a variable rate, which causes minimum payment requirements to fluctuate as rates change. Any significant increase in interest rates may expose the bank to additional credit risk as a marginal customer struggles to make an increased payment.

In addition to credit risk posed by individual borrowers, credit risk also exists in the overall credit card portfolio. Relaxed underwriting standards, aggressive solicitation programs, inadequate account management, as well as a deterioration of general economic conditions, can increase credit risk. Changes in product mix, and the degree to which the portfolio has concentrations, geographic or otherwise, can impact a portfolio's risk profile.

Banks control credit risk through coordinated strategic and marketing plans. They also have comprehensive policies and procedures that include strong front-end controls over underwriting standards, well-defined account management processes, strong back-end controls for effective collection programs, and good management information systems.

Examiners assess credit risk by evaluating portfolio performance, profitability, and customer profiles by business lines, products, and markets. They also consider changes in underwriting standards, account acquisition channels, credit scoring systems, and marketing plans.

Transaction Risk

Transaction risk is the risk to earnings or capital arising from problems with service or product delivery. This risk is a function of internal controls, information systems, employee integrity, and operating processes. Transaction risk exists in all products and services.

A bank's success in credit card lending depends in part on achieving economies of scale. Credit card operations are highly automated, have a large transactional volume, and require strong operational controls. Aggressive growth has the potential to stretch operational capacity and can cause problems in handling customer accounts and in processing payments.

To control transaction risk, a bank should maintain effective internal controls and use comprehensive management information systems.

Examiners assess transaction risk by evaluating the adequacy of credit card application and processing systems and controls. They consider the volume of accounts managed (on the books and securitized), the capabilities of systems and technologies in relation to current and prospective volume, contingency preparedness, and exposures through the payment system.

Liquidity Risk

Liquidity risk is the risk to earnings or capital arising from a bank's inability to meet its obligations when they come due, without incurring unacceptable losses. Liquidity risk includes the inability to manage unplanned decreases or changes in funding sources. Liquidity risk also arises from the failure to recognize or address changes in market conditions that affect the ability to liquidate assets quickly and with minimal loss in value.

Banks use a variety of funding techniques to support credit card portfolios. As such, the techniques individual operations employ have different implications on liquidity risk. For example, a credit card bank self-funded through securitizations (see glossary) has different liquidity risk considerations than a credit card bank funded by its retail parent's commercial paper. Likewise, multinational banks with access to a full array of funding sources to support credit card operations have different liquidity risk considerations.

Liquidity risk is present in a bank's obligation to fund unused credit card commitments. For example, more consumers use their cards at certain times, such as around gift-giving holidays, so the bank must be aware of seasonal demands. Liquidity risk is also present if a bank securitizes its credit card portfolio. Credit card portfolios comprised of higher risk assets and unusual portfolio volatility may be difficult to securitize or sell. Failure to adequately underwrite or collect loans also may trigger early amortization of a securitization, which could cause liquidity problems. Such an event may also increase costs or limit access to funding markets in the future.

Banks control liquidity risk through a strong balance sheet management process, a diversified funding base, a comprehensive liquidity contingency plan, and laddered securitization maturities, if applicable.

To assess liquidity risk, examiners consider:

- The reliability of funding mechanisms.

- The dependence of the credit card operation on securitization of assets.

- The volume of unfunded commitments.

- Attrition of credit card accounts.

- The stability of cobranded and affinity card relationships.

- The ability to fund seasonal demands.

Strategic Risk

Strategic risk is the risk to earnings or capital arising from adverse business decisions or improper implementation of those decisions. This risk is a function of the compatibility between an organization's strategic goals, the business strategies developed to achieve those goals, the resources deployed against these goals, and the quality of implementation. The resources needed to carry out business strategies are both tangible and intangible. They include communication channels, operating systems, delivery networks, and managerial capacities and capabilities.

Strategic risk in credit card lending can arise when business decisions adversely impact the quantity or quality of products, services, operating controls, management supervision, or technology. Management's knowledge of the economic dynamics and market conditions of the industry can help limit strategic risk. For example, banks may be exposed to strategic risk if they inadequately plan or market preapproved credit card solicitation programs. To mitigate the risk, management must fully test new markets, analyze results, and refine solicitation offers to limit the risk of booking new credit card accounts that do not perform as anticipated.

Examiners assess strategic risk by determining whether bank management has evaluated the feasibility and profitability of each new credit card product and service before it is offered. They also determine whether the bank's pricing, growth, and acquisition strategies realistically consider economic and market factors. In particular, examiners evaluate whether a proper balance exists between the bank's willingness to accept risk and its supporting resources and controls.

Reputation Risk

Reputation risk is the risk to earnings or capital arising from negative public opinion. This risk affects the institution's ability to establish new relationships or services, or continue servicing existing relationships. This risk can expose the institution to litigation, financial loss, or damage to its reputation. Reputation risk exposure is present throughout the organization and includes the responsibility to exercise an abundance of caution in dealing with its customers and community. This risk is present in such activities as asset management and agency transactions.

A credit card operation offering an uncompetitive product to the public faces reputation risk because it may be unable to attract new business. In addition, the bank can lose existing relationships if poor service of existing accounts occurs routinely or it does not resolve consumer issues or process payments in a timely manner. Issuing banks often employ outside vendors to perform solicitation, servicing, collections, or other functions and must monitor and control the products and services provided by a third party. Reputation risk also can occur if a bank offers cobranded or affinity credit cards, because consumers may associate the quality of the bank's commercial partner with the bank.

A bank has the responsibility to comply with all consumer laws and regulations. Poor compliance can have a negative affect on the consumers' acceptance of a bank's credit card products.

Poorly underwritten or performing receivables can affect a bank's reputation as an underwriter of credit card securitizations. This creates a risk that future credit enhancements for securitizing credit card receivables may be available at an increased cost or not available at all. Future accessibility to financial markets may be limited or cost more.

Interest Rate Risk

Interest rate risk is the risk to earnings or capital arising from movements in interest rates. The economic perspective focuses on the value of the bank in today's interest rate environment and the sensitivity of that value to changes in interest rates. Interest rate risk arises from differences between the timing of rate changes and the timing of cash flows (repricing risk); from changing rate relationships among different yield curves affecting bank activities (basis risk); from changing rate relationships across the spectrum of maturities (yield curve risk); and from interest related options embedded in bank products (options risk). The evaluation of interest rate risk must consider the impact of complex, illiquid hedging strategies or products, and also the potential impact on fee income, which is sensitive to changes in interest rates. In those situations where trading is separately managed, this refers to structural positions and not trading portfolios.

Interest income derived from credit card portfolios is sensitive to changes in interest rates. The predominance of variable rate pricing and wide spreads, however, provide maximum flexibility in managing such risk. The bank should manage interest rate risk on a consolidated basis for the credit card portfolio and within individual product lines.

When assessing interest rate risk, examiners should consider the variety of pricing programs and the impact of competition on rates. Intense competition on pricing to meet market demands can compress margins. Examiners should also consider the source(s) and cost of funding the credit card portfolio.

Compliance Risk

Compliance risk is the risk to earnings or capital arising from violations or non-conformance with laws, rules, regulations, prescribed practices, or ethical standards. Compliance risk also arises in situations where the laws or rules governing certain bank products or activities of the bank's clients may be ambiguous or untested. Compliance risk exposes the institution to fines, civil money penalties, payment of damages, and the voiding of contracts. Compliance risk can lead to a diminished reputation, reduced franchise value, limited business opportunities, lessened expansion potential, and lack of contract enforceability.

Consumer laws and regulations, including fair lending and other anti-discrimination laws, affect all aspects of credit card lending. Management should ensure that staff involved in credit scoring, processing applications, and collections activity comply fully with these laws and regulations. For their part, examiners should be familiar with fair lending and consumer credit laws and regulations affecting credit card lending. *The Comptroller's Handbook for Compliance* contains detailed guidance on identifying and assessing compliance risk.

Types of Credit Cards

Credit cards can be categorized as falling into two broad categories: general purpose, or bank cards; and proprietary, or private label cards. General purpose cards are sponsored by membership associations and are accepted by many merchants. Private label cards are generally only accepted for purchases at a single retailer.

General Purpose (Bank) Cards

Most banks that offer general purpose cards are members of either Visa or MasterCard, the two primary systems for settling interbank credit card accounts. Visa and MasterCard operate worldwide payment networks among their respective member banks. Banks purchase memberships in the association in return for the ability to offer bank card products and services. The associations require members to conform to their operating policies and procedures to ensure the integrity of the system. They also supply their members with point of sale authorization systems, advertising material, statistical data, industry studies, advisory services, and many other services.

Affinity and Cobranding Programs

Issuers of general purpose bank cards increasingly are forming partnerships with businesses, associations, and not-for-profit groups to market their credit cards. These credit cards, called affinity or cobranded cards, are issued as a MasterCard or Visa. The card can be used for purchases anywhere Visa or MasterCard is accepted as well as for purchase of a partner's products or services, if applicable. A bank issues the card under a contractual agreement with the partner. Although compensation arrangements vary, the partner typically endorses the bank's card in return for a negotiated financial compensation based on an individual's acceptance and use of the card. The cards normally carry the affinity group or cobranding partner's name or logo.

Although the terms cobranded and affinity are sometimes used inter-changeably, there are differences. Affinity cards are issued for a variety of groups or associations, generally not-for-profit organizations, such as alumni associations, professional organizations, sports enthusiasts, etc. They provide cardholders access to credit and a way to identify with the group. The affinity group is compensated for endorsing the issuer's card. Compensation can include a portion of annual card fees, fees paid upon renewal, a percentage of the interchange income, or a share of the interest income. The group is able to receive income without much expense. The issuing bank benefits because the association's endorsement introduces the bank to what it hopes is a high quality customer list. Members of affinity groups also are typically more responsive to credit card solicitations than other consumers are to generic cards, allowing the issuer to better target marketing initiatives.

In a cobranded card program, an issuing bank forms a partnership with a for-profit organization. Cobranded partners of issuing banks include for-profit organizations such as hotels, gas companies, automobile manufacturers, or airlines. The cobranding partner may receive part of the income that would normally go to the issuer, such as part of the interchange income. The partner also benefits because the issuer brings customer service and expertise in consumer lending to the partnership.

A bank card issuer benefits from a cobranding program because it increases credit card receivables. Holders of such cards tend to use their card more often than traditional card holders because the nonbank partner typically offers them financial rewards, such as discounts or rebates, as an enticement for using the card. (See the section in this introduction entitled "Reserving for Rebate Programs" for a discussion of risks associated with rebates.)

Issuing banks should not materially modify underwriting standards, account management activities, and collection practices that are important to safety and soundness simply to accommodate prospective affinity or cobranded card customers. These programs are essentially marketing strategies. Examiners should review and discuss with management any modifications to terms, account management activities, or collection practices to determine that any such impact on portfolio quality does not serve as the basis for a safety and soundness problem.

Issuers with numerous accounts tied to affinity or cobranded programs can be seriously impacted by their partners' viability and commitment to the program. Bank management should thoroughly analyze partners in such credit card programs before finalizing contracts. Negative publicity about the partner could reflect poorly on the bank. The bank issuer of affinity cards should obtain verification from an independent source that the group is legitimate. Management also should determine the financial status of its cobranding partner. The bank may be exposed to liability for unpaid rebates if the partner is not financially sound.

Contract terms should specify that control over the partnership rests with the issuer. Issuers should track and monitor the performance of each partnership program, including response and approval rates, utilization rates, purchase volume, delinquencies, charge-offs, etc. The bank's planning strategies should factor in the possibility of high attrition rates if such a group or business withdraws its endorsement from the bank.

Corporate Cards

The corporate credit card is another type of general purpose card. The bank issues corporate cards to selected employees of the sponsoring company. Generally, employees use the cards for travel and entertainment expenses incurred on behalf of the company. The terms of the contract between the bank and sponsoring company dictate whether the company will guarantee employees' credit card loans, whether and how the bank will set credit limits for the company and its employees, and whether the bank will specify repayment terms, etc. Corporate programs may also include other services, such as travel insurance and record keeping.

Some bank corporate card departments also offer a related product known as a procurement account. The bank issues the corporation a Visa/MasterCard account which can be used to purchase items ranging from office supplies to rocket engines. The credit limits on these accounts can exceed several million dollars, depending upon the needs of the corporation. These accounts generally pay the balance monthly and do not typically revolve. A bank may incur costs associated with carrying the loan if the corporation does not pay its balance when billed.

Corporate cards are generally less profitable to banks than consumer credit cards because they do not routinely incur finance charges. Rather, annual fees, interchange income, and other service fees are the primary sources of income. As a result, banks should closely analyze the costs and risks associated with such programs and have the necessary expertise before engaging in the business.

Depending upon how the program is structured, corporate card programs may pose more commercial credit risk to the bank than consumer credit risk because the company is the source of repayment. In such cases, the bank must assess the initial and ongoing financial condition of the company in its underwriting decision and assign credit risk ratings consistent with the internal rating of the commercial credit.

Management and examiners should check for possible concentrations of credit (aggregate of company card lines) and legal lending limit implications (card lines combined with commercial and other loans to the company). They also should review corporate procurement cards that revolve, as the credit line may become an unintended working capital loan to the company.

The extent of initial and ongoing review of employees' creditworthiness should be based upon the sponsoring company's liability for repayment of the employees' debt.

Secured Credit Cards

Secured credit cards are general purpose credit cards targeted to customers with poor or limited credit histories who do not qualify for a traditional, unsecured credit card loan. These programs benefit consumers by helping them either establish or reestablish a satisfactory credit history. If these customers perform satisfactorily, many banks will "graduate" them to an unsecured credit card.

Secured credit cards are collateralized by cash deposits, generally a passbook savings account or certificate of deposit. Depending upon the bank's policy, the credit limit is 50 percent to 100 percent of the deposit amount. The bank may pay interest on the deposit account. Secured card programs are attractive to the bank for several reasons:

- Credit risk is significantly reduced because the collateral is liquid.

- The asset is self-funding.

- The market for secured credit cards has not been saturated.

- Annual fees and finance charges are often higher than on traditional unsecured cards; the issuer also may impose other charges such as an application or processing fee.

- The product allows the bank to access a new population of bank customers with minimal risk.

While risks may seem to be mitigated with secured credit cards, banks still incur transaction and credit risk. Some banks have incurred substantial losses in their secured credit card portfolios because they have failed to monitor deposit account balances, monitor the activities of independent service organizations (ISOs) (see glossary), or control the practices of consumers charging over credit limits. Proper controls and account monitoring are essential to successful secured card programs.

The bank also should establish clear underwriting criteria. Ordinarily, a complete credit analysis of all applicants should be performed, including obtaining credit bureau reports, if available, and verifying income.

Secured card programs raise unique consumer compliance and security perfection issues. For instance, common law gives banks a general right to offset the loan balance against any customer deposits held by the bank. In a credit card transaction, however, Regulation Z prohibits a bank from offsetting card holder deposits unless it has a security interest in the cardholder's deposit account. The bank should consult with legal counsel to ensure notes and security agreements comply with consumer regulations and protect the bank's security interest.

Private Label Cards

Private label cards are issued under a contractual agreement between a bank and a retailer, such as a department store, or another commercial firm, such as an oil company. Private label cards typically differ from general purpose cards because they limit where the card is accepted, they generally have lower credit limits, and cardholders often exhibit a higher risk profile.

Private label cards programs are attractive to banks because they provide an opportunity to tap new revolving credit markets. Banks also may use these programs as leverage to expand or establish new commercial relationships. A private label card is attractive to retailers because it promotes sales and customer loyalty.

When evaluating whether to offer private label cards, a bank should review carefully the financial condition of its retail partner. For example, a retailer that wants to maximize the number of cards in circulation may ask the bank to lower its credit standards. If the bank agrees, it should ensure that the retailer is liable for ensuing losses and that it has the financial capacity to meet this liability. Also, if a retailer declares bankruptcy, private label cardholders may not feel compelled to repay the unpaid balances. The bank should have procedures in place to analyze and respond to such contingencies.

Overall Management and Oversight

Credit card lending is a highly automated and high volume activity that distributes sophisticated products to consumers. The credit card operation should have the management and organizational structure, expertise, staffing levels, information systems, training programs, and audit processes to be effective within this environment. Accountability and responsibility must be clearly defined at every level.

A bank's strategy for credit card activities should identify, in broad terms, the level of risk it is willing to accept for various products in its portfolio. The plan should reflect realistic goals and objectives based on reasonable data and assumptions. The bank's appetite for risk often involves balancing underwriting and the pricing structure to achieve desired results. For example, a bank may ease its credit standards in return for a higher interest rate, projecting increased profits in spite of higher losses, which may be associated with those accounts. The examiner should assess the adequacy of the total strategy.

All banks must implement sound fundamental principles, which identify risk, establish controls, and provide for monitoring systems for lending activities. Because credit card lending includes numerous activities that pose significant risks, the bank should have effective policies and strong internal controls governing each operational area. Effective policies and internal controls enable the bank to adhere to its established strategic objectives and to institutionalize effective risk management practices. Policies also can help ensure that the bank benefits through efficiencies gained from standard operating procedures.

The requirement for effective policies and internal controls does not alter a bank's designation as noncomplex. The OCC, however, requires banks to have written policies covering their credit card operations unless the risk in their activity is so small that it is considered *de minimis*.

Risk Management Control Systems

Control systems identify, measure, and monitor risks. These systems include audit, loan review, and risk management. The structure and function can vary depending on the size and complexity of credit card operations. The technology, level of sophistication, and staffing levels also may be different. The examiner must determine how and where the function is performed, and assess its effectiveness.

The bank's audit and loan review functions should review the credit card operation. Audit procedures should include regular testing of the credit underwriting function for compliance with policy guidelines, and review of all significant policies for prudence and staff adherence to policy. The examiner should evaluate the effect of the absence of an audit or loan review function on a credit card operation and discuss with management.

Just as in the commercial credit area of the bank, a strong credit risk management function is crucial to the ongoing success and profitability of the credit card operation. The risk management function is responsible for evaluating credit standards, monitoring the quality of the portfolio, and making changes to the underwriting standards as necessary to maintain the appropriate level of risk in the portfolio. The risk management function promotes early and accurate identification of existing and potential problems, identifies the need for policy revisions, and provides management with the information it needs to respond promptly to changes.

The risk management process should address the entire cycle of credit card lending, from strategic development, testing, product roll out, and continuing into long-term performance of the portfolio. At a minimum, the risk management function should include responsibility for performing product analyses to serve as the basis for underwriting, marketing, and portfolio management decisions. It should ensure that marketing initiatives appropriately reflect acceptable levels of risk. Risk management should help manage and maintain all scoring systems, analyze portfolio delinquencies and losses, and identify reasons for adverse changes or trends. It should also monitor portfolio performance, including the performance of specific products, marketing initiatives, vintage (see glossary), etc.

The bank should have adequate management information systems (MIS) in place to perform its risk management functions effectively. For example, MIS should be able to provide sufficient information to evaluate and measure the impact of actions taken. Senior management should receive reports derived from MIS data outlining portfolio dimensions, composition, and performance. Reports should include portfolio risk levels, trends, concentrations, and earnings.

Scoring Models

Scoring models, or scorecards, are tools used to predict the behavior of new applicants based on the performance of previous applicants. They rank order applicants or customers by risk based upon the information consumers supply in credit applications and credit bureau reports on payment history. The points for each scorable component are added, producing a score which rank orders the applicants along a risk ladder (the score scale).

Although some institutions develop their own scoring models, most are built by outside vendors. Vendors build scoring models based upon specific information and parameters provided by bank management. Management, therefore, must clearly communicate with the vendor and ensure that the scorecard developer clearly understands the bank's objectives.

Data used to develop the scorecard can come from three sources: a bank's previous good accounts, bad accounts, and rejected applicants; pooled data (purchased data whose characteristics closely resemble applicants which the bank desires); and expert intelligence (the logic and evaluation processes used by successful loan officers). More reliable scores result when the company's own experience from samples of good accounts, bad accounts, and rejected applicants forms the basis for the scorecards. Pooled data scores also may be effective, however, when a company's own experience is not available.

An effective scoring model should predict the likelihood with 95 percent confidence that the model will separate "good" and "bad" accounts. Although each bank decides its definition of "good" and "bad," many banks use 90-days delinquent or the likelihood that an account will go bankrupt within a certain period of time as a definition of "bad." This enables management to make the decision to grant or deny credit according to a previously established corporate policy on acceptable credit risk.

If scoring models are used, the bank should test whether the model predicts risk effectively for its own accounts. Management should periodically evaluate the accuracy of the scoring model to determine whether it continues to perform as intended. When the scoring model does not perform as intended, the bank may need to develop a new scorecard.

Management should provide credit scoring guidance to staff. This guidance could include: procedures for documented audit trails, documentation retention guidelines, internal controls that prohibit manipulation of the scorecards, reporting guidelines, and override and exception guidelines. The guidance should be reviewed and updated as necessary.

There are distinct types of scoring models: application, credit bureau risk score, credit bureau bankruptcy score, credit bureau revenue score, behavior, collections, payment projection, and recovery. (See Appendix A for more information on various scoring models.)

Advantages and Disadvantages of Credit Scoring

The advantages to credit scoring are:

- Controlling approval rates B Credit scoring gives bank management the ability to control approval and acquisition rates while maintaining the present loss rate. It allows management to better assess a customer who is slightly outside the specified credit criteria. Credit scoring also is an effective quality control mechanism for reducing volume during adverse economic periods.

- Reducing credit losses B Use of credit scoring may reduce the credit loss rate, depending on how well credit decisions were made prior to the use of a credit scoring system.

- Expanding customer demographics B Credit scoring provides descriptive statistics about potential customers that are useful in analyzing the target market profile, measuring the effectiveness of current sales and marketing efforts, and improving the solicitation and/or advertising strategy.

- Evaluating new programs B Credit scoring provides quantifiable information on expected delinquency and loss rates. These rates can be compared with those of the existing portfolios to forecast performance of new programs. Also, in rapid growth situations, credit scoring, with its weighting formula of customer attributes, can establish a risk profile of new programs that can then be compared with prior experience.

- Processing efficiency B Credit scoring can reduce the number of credit bureau reports required, the number of credit analysts required, and processing time.

- Validating the effect of credit criteria B Credit scoring allows the accuracy of a score to be monitored. If scoring results in the bank accepting more risk than it wants, the cutoff score can be adjusted or the model rebuilt.

- Managing the portfolio B New account credit scoring also can be used to improve initial credit line assignment decisions and to assess credit performance early in the account life cycle, when remedial action can be most effective.

Disadvantages associated with credit scoring are:

- The scorecards may not reflect and meet the bank's credit risk management objectives (often balanced with marketing objectives), particularly as they change.

- The scorecards may rely on inaccurate or unreliable data from credit bureaus.

- The scorecards may not be adequately monitored through available management information. Management must review credit override and exception reports daily, monitor performance results and trends by score level, and implement controls as appropriate.

- Management may fail to provide adequate and effective user training to promote system usage according to policy.

- The scoring system may not adequately incorporate compliance effects test issues. Even when a lender applies a policy or practice equally to credit applicants, the policy or practice could have a disproportionate adverse impact on applicants from a group protected against discrimination. If that occurs, the policy or practice is described as having a "disparate impact or effect." Management should ensure that the bank's scorecards do not have the effect of discrimination.

- Credit scoring may lull management into a false sense of security about its portfolio. However good scoring models are, they are not perfect and may prove to be inaccurate for a variety of reasons, including changes in credit card lending and repayment patterns. Hence it is incumbent upon management to monitor its credit scoring strategies closely.

Cutoff Score

Scoring models do not make credit decisions. Rather, management implements its underwriting policy by setting one or more cutoff scores for use in the credit decision making process. In some banks, the score serves as the definitive approve/decline process. Most banks, however, also perform a judgmental review of all loans within a set number of points of the cutoff for which potential customers above a set score are approved and those below are declined. Examiners should focus their attention on this gray area.

These cutoff scores may be changed by bank management, which alters the risk profile of the originated loans. The cutoff score is the control mechanism for volume (quantity) and profit (quality) in loans. As a basic principle, the higher the cutoff score, the lower the approval rate and delinquency problems. Decisions to change the cutoff score reflect a change of strategy, a change in quality of applications or names for solicitations, or more insight into the market and its profitability. (See Appendix A for more detail on cutoff score strategies.)

Overrides

For automated systems, underwriting exceptions are termed "overrides." An override is a decision to accept or reject an applicant when the scorecard says otherwise. High-side overrides and low-side overrides exist. With a high-side override, the bank rejects an applicant which the scorecard would approve. A high-side override can occur when the bank considers variables or characteristics which were excluded from the model. With a low-side override, the bank approves an applicant which the scorecard would reject. An excessive level of overrides, either high-side or low-side, negates the use of scoring models. If the scoring model properly reflects the bank's risk parameters, overrides should be used with considerable caution.

The three types of overrides are policy, informational, and intuitive. Policy overrides occur when management sets up special rules for some kinds of applications. Informational overrides are based on information not available in the scorecard or only available in small quantities, like other existing customer accounts. Intuitive overrides are based on "gut feeling." Management should have the ability to identify the volume and track the effectiveness of overrides.

Typically, the override rate is calculated by comparing the number of overrides, either high-side or low-side, to the number of applications in that population. For the high-side override rate, compare the number of applicants over the cutoff score who were denied to the number of applicants over the cutoff score. For the low-side override rate, compare the number of applicants below the cutoff score who were accepted to the number of applications below the cutoff score. A large number of overrides is equivalent to having no cutoff at all and jeopardizes the bank's ability to measure the predictability of the scoring system. When override rates are more than what the scoring manual provided by the vendor or developed by the bank deems reasonable, the examiner should evaluate the override policy and discuss any concerns with management.

MIS for Credit Scoring Systems

To manage the risks associated with scorecards, bank management should periodically review a group of management information reports. The reports include the population stability report, the characteristic analysis report, the final score report, the delinquency report, and the portfolio chronology log. (See Appendix A for more detail on these reports.)

Validation and Redevelopment

For generic cards or bureau scores, the vendor is responsible for validating the scorecard. This should be done on a regular basis. The bank is responsible for ensuring that its population is similar to that of the development sample.

Custom built scoring models should be statistically validated on the bank's most recent data prior to implementation to confirm the model's ability to rank order risk as designed. The validation process ensures that the profile of current applicants, or names for prescreening, is similar to that used in the development sample. The monitoring reports described in Appendix A can be used to validate the system.

After a reasonable implementation period (six to eight months on a credit card scoring model, although banks without sufficient volume may need to wait longer before fully validating the model), revalidating the scoring models should be done as needed to keep the system statistically sound. The frequency of the revalidation analysis will depend upon the volume of applications received or solicitations offered. In the revalidation process, the bank or outside vendor is taking a recent sample of accepted and rejected applications, rescoring them, and comparing the performance of that sample to the development sample to ensure the model is still rank ordering risk the same.

Additionally, banks should be generating the tracking reports detailed in Appendix A to perform periodic monitoring of their scorecards. In a small bank this may be done semiannually or annually. In a large bank, quarterly, or even monthly, monitoring of the reports which track the scores and vintage of the population will help determine when the scorecard is losing its predictive ability.

In banks where the characteristics of the applicant population are not changing and no other changes are occurring, the scorecard may continue to be predictive for five to seven years, possibly longer. In other banks where customer demographics are changing rapidly, a new scorecard may need to be redeveloped within two to three years.

Marketing and Underwriting of New Accounts

The competition in the credit card industry, combined with the relative saturation of the market, make new account acquisition a key component of a successful credit card operation. Marketing for new accounts has evolved from a relatively simple process of offering credit cards to existing bank customers through "take-one" applications in branches to a highly sophisticated operation that selectively places the product in households throughout a large, often nationwide market. Increased penetration from these marketing enhancements has also brought profitable cross-selling opportunities to banks.

But marketing is expensive, and not without risks. Even successful marketing programs can leave the bank with a new population of customers with higher risk profiles than the bank would initially want. A bank's involvement in marketing depends primarily upon its size, strategic and growth plans, appetite for risk, and distribution network. Management must, therefore, clearly define and control its marketing process. The bank's marketing activities should be guided by a detailed, realistic marketing plan which is consistent with the overall goals and objectives of the bank's strategic plan. Policies and procedures should ensure that other functional areas of the bank (e.g., credit risk management, operations, systems, legal, compliance) are adequately involved in all aspects of the marketing process. Other necessary components of a successful marketing operation include experienced and competent management and staff, reliable projections and market analyses, and complete and accurate MIS reports, often by product and initiative.

Credit card issuers acquire new accounts by **preapproved solicitations**, through approval of completed **applications**, and through **portfolio acquisitions** from third parties. These are three very distinct acquisition methods. All require sound underwriting practices to achieve and maintain the desired portfolio quality.

Preapproved Solicitations

In a preapproved solicitation program, a credit card issuer uses a list of potential customers from which it will make a firm offer of credit. Compiling the list of names is typically a joint effort involving the bank's marketing and risk management function or credit divisions. Marketing is usually responsible for identifying the targeted population, creating the products the bank will offer, and controlling marketing costs. The risk management function's main responsibilities include establishing the prescreening credit criteria, establishing credit lines, and monitoring the success of the program after the accounts are booked. The area in the bank responsible for the finances of the credit card operation may play a key role in projecting the impact that credit and marketing decisions will have on the profitability of new accounts obtained through preapproved solicitations.

Before proceeding with any preapproved solicitation program, the bank should ensure that it has the systems necessary to capture needed data once accounts are booked. For example, systems may need to capture credit bureau scores, number of respondents, and reasons why, once approved, an applicant's credit declines.

Credit card issuers usually plan preapproved campaigns throughout the year to obtain new accounts. They may either purchase a list(s) of names from a list vendor and/or the credit bureaus or they may identify a segment of the bank's borrowers. Lists purchased from outside vendors are assigned to the credit bureaus to start the prescreening process after the bank gives the credit bureaus written instructions of its approved prescreen criteria. Banks generally specify two types of criteria: exclusion and credit.

Exclusion criteria eliminate prospects that the bank does not want to consider in the mailing. These prospects are not scored. Persons with serious, derogatory credit histories are examples of excluded prospects.

Credit criteria are subsequently used to subdivide the remaining prospects into different groups. Issuers commonly incorporate credit bureau scores into these levels of credit criteria. This allows them to target score ranges with estimated good/bad probability rates. The different criteria levels allow the bank to select the overall risk profile it desires and offer variations in the product and pricing based on risk. Prospects usually are categorized into level A, B, etc., with A being the lowest risk. Those that fail level A criteria are considered for level B, those that fail B will move onto C, etc. The last level contains consumers who did not fit within the higher levels, yet still passed the general exclusion criteria.

A bank also establishes criteria for credit line assignments. Some banks assign the credit line up front, which is then disclosed to the consumer as part of the preapproved offer. Another common approach is for banks to offer the consumer a credit limit up to a certain amount. The bank does not assign the line until after the consumer responds to the solicitation. The criteria that the banks use will vary, but may be based on a combination of disclosed income and credit bureau score and/or criteria level.

Once the bureau prescreens the list of prospects against the bank's criteria, the bank has the opportunity to review the breakdown by criteria level. The information the bank receives at this point does not have identifying information about the consumers, such as names and addresses. This is done to avoid triggering provisions of the Fair Credit Reporting Act. Therefore, the bank can still eliminate prospects if it wants to reduce the size of its overall mailing or the number of consumers solicited within a certain criteria level.

The Comptroller's compliance booklets describe the Fair Credit Reporting Act and provide guidance on a bank's ability to deny credit to consumers targeted in a preapproved solicitation campaign. With very limited exceptions, once the bank receives the list with prospect names and other identifying information, it must make a firm offer of credit to each consumer on the list. As a result, the bank must ensure that the list is based on the criteria that it submitted to the credit bureaus and list processors. For example, the bank should complete audits to ensure that the credit bureaus applied the correct credit criteria. The bank should complete this audit after the credit bureau prescreening, but before taking delivery of the names.

Many banks use a third-party list processor throughout the prescreening process. The list processor performs various steps, which include eliminating duplicate names and existing cardholders and verifying addresses. The bank may also use scoring models to help identify consumers who would be more likely to respond and provide more income to the bank by revolving their balances.

After the bank receives the names, it solicits the consumer by direct mail, telemarketing, or both. The bank or a third party then processes the responses. The bank may get updated credit bureau information for a portion of the responders as a "back-end" audit to verify that the characteristics of the responders match expectations. Some banks obtain updated credit bureau information on all responders to determine if there has been a significant change in the responder's credit history.

Once the bank books the new accounts, those performing the risk management function should analyze the results and determine the characteristics of the responders. They should determine whether the bank was successful in attracting the types of consumers it targeted.

The risk management function continues to play an important role in monitoring the performance of the portfolio, as the results of previous preapproved solicitations provide valuable information for future programs. One method used to analyze results is to complete a vintage analysis. Management may organize vintages by "campaign" or by quarterly or annual periods. At a minimum, vintage reports should include delinquency and credit loss information. A more comprehensive set of vintage reporting would include bankruptcy, activation, utilization, and attrition information. Vintage reports are an effective way to compare the performance of various segments of the portfolio, based on the origination period and acquisition method. The reports also can be used to compare actual to projected performance. The risk management function should determine the reason for any significant differences.

As mentioned previously, risk management normally helps establish credit criteria and performs projections before the preapproved solicitation campaign. Risk management also should promptly and thoroughly analyze the results of major preapproved solicitation programs. The function should first review the results of preapproved solicitations within a relatively short time frame, such as three months, to determine the quality and quantity of responders and whether or not the preapproved solicitation attracted the desired account holders. Shortly thereafter, risk management should review activation rates, balances, and delinquencies. For the next six months to a year, it should review the financial results of each major preapproved solicitation and compare these results to the initial forecasts. Risk management also should continue to track all major preapproved solicitations in order to prepare reports, which may include annualized vintage comparisons, segment/product comparisons, and other items of interest.

An effective account acquisition program will require testing changes in credit standards and marketing practices before full rollout. A bank's testing program should have defined objectives and requirements for analysis, review, and decision making. A bank may perform a wide variety of tests to evaluate variables, such as changes in criteria, cutoff scores, and pricing and product type.

For example, assume the bank plans to solicit 1,000 names for a preapproved offering. One test may include allowing 50 of those solicited to have two 60-day delinquencies on credit reports within the previous 12 months, even though this population would normally be excluded. These 50 are the test group. The remaining 950 solicited would be the control group. Management would then monitor the test group's performance in relation to the control group until it can reach a reasonable conclusion about the effect of the change in delinquency standards. The time period for the test will vary, depending upon the nature of the test. It may take up to 18 months before a bank can make a valid conclusion regarding changes to credit criteria, however.

Applications

Banks market credit card applications in various ways including direct mail, telemarketing, magazine inserts, and counter top "take-one" applications. A consumer completes an application and sends it to the bank for processing. Some banks use an automated application processing system to process applications. An analyst keys in information from the application and a credit bureau report is automatically obtained. The bank must have a system in place to ensure that data from the applications is inputted correctly.

The bank may use a judgmental process, an automated scoring system, or a combination of both to grant credit. Regardless of the method employed, management should have well-defined guidelines for the credit approval process.

As noted above, when credit scoring is used to grant credit, quality is controlled by setting the cutoff score at the desired loss rate. When a credit decision is made judgmentally, the bank controls the quality of new accounts by establishing well-understood credit guidelines within its policy. The bank must have control systems in place to ensure that analysts consistently follow the policy.

Portfolio Acquisitions

Investors acquire credit card portfolios for many reasons. They may want to quickly expand an already established credit card business, realize improved economies of scale, diversify product lines/niches and geographic markets, and increase profits. A seller, on the other hand, may wish to reinvest in other investments, recapitalize its business, or increase liquidity. Whatever the reason, there are markets for credit card portfolios and the premiums can be lucrative for general purpose bank card product lines. Private label card programs are valued very differently and may even be purchased at a discount.

Banks should have procedures, systems, and controls in place to govern portfolio acquisitions. Procedures provide consistent analysis throughout the acquisition process and reduce the risk that a critical item or aspect of the transaction will be overlooked. The procedures should incorporate detailed instructions regarding such areas as prospective portfolio reviews, due diligence, and final analysis. (See the "Purchased Credit Card Relationships" section of this introduction and Appendix D for a discussion of intangible assets resulting from credit card portfolio acquisitions.)

Account Management

Credit card account holders' financial situations and needs change over time, both for the better and for the worse. The challenge is to identify and respond to those changes promptly and appropriately. This is the role of the account management function. While the terms used for this function may differ among banks, the intent remains the same: add value to the card holder for the bank, thereby maximizing lending opportunities, and controlling credit and/or fraud losses.

Account management practices cover various activities, but they typically have one thing in common. Like the original approval decision, they affect how much and for what period of time the bank makes credit available to the customer.

Account management activities include credit line increases and decreases, card renewals/reissuances, payment holidays, and overlimit authorizations. For problem accounts, account management activities include decisions to "block" code accounts, i.e., withdraw or limit charging privileges. These activities are discussed separately in the "Collections" section of this introduction.

A bank must implement effective monitoring, information systems, and account management strategies to administer its credit card portfolio. These portfolios generally consist of large volumes of open-end lines of credit to cardholders who are not typically obligated to supply financial information after their accounts are opened. The processes and programs employed, and the level of automation and technology involved, will vary. The examiner must evaluate account management programs and the corresponding policies and procedures in place for appropriateness given the individual issuer's circumstances. The examiner also should assess the tools, systems, and available MIS to ensure they provide the bank with necessary and timely information.

To make prudent credit decisions, issuers need to maintain a current credit risk profile for their card holder bases. Large issuers typically accomplish this through regular application of behavioral scoring to the card holder base. Some banks use behavioral scores in conjunction with credit bureau scores to further enhance account screening techniques. Due to the expense involved, smaller issuers often do not use automated behavioral scoring systems. Nevertheless, they need to have some process in place to assess ongoing card holder credit risk in order to make timely and prudent account management decisions.

Many issuers use automated account management strategies.

The advantage to automated strategies lies largely in their ability to implement credit decisions for large numbers of accounts with minimal manual intervention. In developing such strategies, management will make a determination of card holder characteristics that warrant particular treatment (e.g., automatic 20 percent line increases, 10 percent overlimit approvals, etc.). Once automated, only the exceptions C those which exceed strategy specifications or accounts which did not meet strategy specifications C will need manual review. This can significantly reduce costs.

The issuer also may opt to run "champion/challenger" scenarios to continue to refine its account management

strategies. In a champion/challenger strategy, management applies one strategy against a portion of the portfolio (champion) and other strategies (challengers) against additional segments of the portfolio to identify a more successful practice. For example, management may decide to explore the impact of changing the amount of automatic line increases. Objectives for such a move could include improving line utilization, increasing card holder retention, or increasing revolving balances. To test their impact, management might apply one line increase strategy against 85 percent of the eligible accounts (champion), and three other strategies (challengers) against each of the other 5 percent segments. The champion may provide for 20 percent line increases at one-year intervals (up to a cap), and the challengers may offer 15 percent, 25 percent, and no increases. If one of the challengers proves more effective than the champion in meeting the bank's objectives, management may substitute the challenger percentage for the champion. The examiner should ensure that management adequately tests a given challenger series and thoroughly weighs the costs/benefits before placing it in a champion position.

Although marketing typically drives the timing of the various account management initiatives, the risk management/credit policy function should establish the credit criteria used. Smaller programs often require authorization by the risk management or credit policy function. If the program involves extending a significant amount of credit or diverting from established underwriting guidelines or philosophies, however, senior management should review and approve changes before implementation.

The following sections discuss commonly used account management practices.

Authorizations

Authorization is the process whereby the card issuer approves a credit card transaction for a given account. The key is to ensure that the authorization system allows good customers to make transactions within preset limits, while preventing transactions that pose undue credit risk to the bank.

Authorization processes vary among banks, with some incorporating the use of champion/challenger strategies. Regardless of the specific processes used, policies and procedures that reflect the bank's risk tolerance should guide the entire authorization process. Management also should ensure that there are mechanisms in place to monitor adherence to those policies and procedures, and to ensure data integrity. Key management reports will detail the number and dollar volume of overlimit accounts, severely overlimit accounts, and authorization policy exceptions.

Merchants process transactions differently, resulting in differences in the level of manual intervention required by the issuer in the authorization process. Some merchants clear their sales using paper sales drafts or transmit sales information via a dial terminal, both of which require a higher level of manual authorization. The vast majority of merchants, however, submit their sales information electronically via electronic data capture (EDC) networks established by Visa and MasterCard. Combined with technologically advanced merchant terminals, these networks enable virtually immediate authorizations for the vast majority of transactions at the point of sale.

In a typical electronic sales transaction, the salesperson passes the credit card through an electronic card reader. The merchant processor's system records the information from the card's magnetic strip and transmits the transaction information through the Visa or MasterCard network to the issuing bank for authorization. The issuing bank generally automatically authorizes the transaction unless the purchase results in an overlimit situation beyond preset percentages or dollar amounts or information available to the issuer suggests potential fraud. In those cases, direct contact with the issuing bank is required. These "manual" authorizations are usually routed to the customer service unit of the issuing bank. (See the "Fraud Control" section in this introduction.)

As in other areas, the examiner should determine that changes to authorization guidelines are based on sound analyses of their potential impact, and that the bank adequately tracks and analyzes the impact of previous changes. The bank should regularly review and update the credit criteria used for authorization decisions.

Credit Line Increases

Credit card issuers strive to maximize profitability. With that in mind, the bank will attempt to maximize credit lines commensurate with card holder risk profiles. Some studies show, in part, that a cardholder's decision regarding which credit card to use and/or retain may well depend on the credit line available. Given this and the profitability potential, issuers generally try to offer the highest lines possible. But the issuer must balance the potential rewards with the risks. Therefore, it is critical that the issuer base its credit line decisions on sound credit information, including payment history.

Some card issuers may grant conditional line increases, i.e., conditioned on the card holder cashing a check provided by the issuer. If the card holder uses the check, the issuer automatically increases the cardholder's line. If not used within a set time period, 30 or 60 days for example, the issuer withdraws the offer and the available line does not change. Issuers use this program to build receivables and possibly to encourage customers to pay off lines with other banks (similar to balance transfer programs offered at account origination). The bank's guidelines for this activity should include eligibility criteria similar to those required for regular line increase programs.

Line increase and decrease decisions occur through bank-initiated, system wide programs or customer-initiated requests. Issuers with automated line increase programs use various scoring models (behavioral, credit, etc.) to screen the card holder base. The issuer periodically applies the scoring models to the card holder base, identifying accounts eligible for line increases or decreases. The automated line increase system then combines scores with other qualifying criteria, such as time elapsed since the last line increase, and makes line increase assignments accordingly. Issuers sometimes use champion/challenger scenarios in this process.

With customer-initiated requests, the issuer considers each request as received. The bank's policy and procedures should clearly establish approval criteria, specify the approval process, define customer verification steps, assign responsibility, establish lending authorities, and outline documentation requirements. Depending upon the process in place, credit analysts generally review customer-initiated requests manually. In some cases, customer service representatives may handle small emergency line increase requests.

Issuers should not normally grant line increases for accounts that score below cutoffs and/or otherwise fail underwriting criteria. For example, banks often exclude accounts with recent or serious delinquencies, prior bankruptcy or charge-off experience, and new accounts from line increase programs or decisions. Management should ensure clear understanding of the exception process, including approval and documentation requirements. Management also should review comprehensive exception reports on a regular basis.

Reissues/Renewals

Banks issue credit card accounts with pre-set expiration dates, typically two or three years. These expiration dates provide the issuer with the opportunity to determine whether or not to continue the relationship. The bank uses scoring models and/or established credit guidelines for this process. The guidelines should consider the age of the account, utilization rate, average balance carried, delinquency status, payment history, and, if available, account profitability. Based upon this information, the issuer makes a decision to renew or not to renew the card. If renewed, the issuer decides whether the credit limit will stay the same or go up or down. The issuer also may use this information to adjust the reissue expiration date.

This process is usually automated, therefore applied uniformly to a large number of accounts. As such, the issuer should have processes in place which test reissue decisions to determine that the system is operating as designed and to evaluate the effectiveness of reissue strategies.

Payment Deferral Plans

Many card issuers offer customers the opportunity to skip or defer normally scheduled minimum monthly payments, commonly known as "payment holiday" or "skip payment" programs. The card issuer benefits from these programs because customers continue to carry balances and interest continues to accrue. Customers can use these grace periods to defer their debt repayment.

Banks notify selected cardholders of such programs via statement inserts or printed messages on monthly statements. Marketing often times these offers to coincide with heavy purchasing periods such as August (vacations and back-to-school spending) and December (holiday spending).

Banks should have procedures which ensure that they only offer skip payment programs to customers, which the bank has reason to believe, will not abuse this opportunity and create safety and soundness problems. As with other account management decisions, the risk management or credit policy functions should set the criteria used to select eligible accounts.

"Pay ahead" programs differ from "payment holidays" and "skip payment" plans in that they require the card holder to "pay" for future payment waivers. Essentially, the bank applies the payment amount which exceeds the cardholder's minimum payment toward future payments. The card holder enjoys a zero minimum balance due until the credit is exhausted. While the practice does not constitute a problem in and of itself, it does impair the bank's ability to identify problem accounts on a timely basis. Therefore, banks using this program should clearly define how many minimum payments a card holder can "waive" with a lump sum payment.

The bank must have a process in place to regularly review the performance of the accounts which accept skip payment/payment deferral programs. Analyses should address such issues as acceptance trends, line utilization, and the ultimate impact of such programs on delinquency status and credit losses. These analyses should then form the bases for defining future offerings.

Collections

Bad debt and fraud losses in credit cards have risen sharply in recent years when compared with historical levels. Reasons for increased losses include changes in underwriting standards, continued mass marketing of cards in a saturated market, escalation of consumer bankruptcy, and economic stagnation in certain geographic regions. Also, collection systems and controls have not always kept pace with new account generation.

An effective collection process is a key component of controlling and minimizing credit losses. It must be managed effectively at each operational level. The problems associated with an inadequately managed collection function include:

- Reduced earnings caused by increased loan losses and reduced recoveries.

- Inaccurate or untimely communications to senior management and the directorate.

- Inaccurate reporting of past due and charged off loans, and possibly imprudent management decisions.

- Improper use of reaging (changing the delinquency status of an account), fixed payment/workout programs, or other collection practices.

- Insufficient allowance for loan losses caused by weak MIS, inaccurate past due figures, and the improper use of reaging, fixed payment programs, etc.

- Inadequate audit trail of collection and recovery activities.

- Poorly trained employees, resulting in loss of productivity, collections, and recoveries.

- Violations of law and regulations.

The collection function is increasingly difficult to manage properly due to the growing size and complexity of the credit card issuing business and collection's labor-intensive nature. Consequently, the use of specialized, state-of-the-art technology is increasingly required to optimize productivity and control overhead costs. Management uses the technology and current and historical information at its disposal to formulate a plan or strategy for optimizing its collection efforts. In general, the strategy will attempt to direct the department's efforts to those accounts with the greatest risk of loss and the greatest potential for collection.

The philosophies and structures of collection departments can vary significantly. But they have one thing in common: the need to closely supervise the collection staff. Under normal conditions, the ratio of collectors to supervisors usually does not exceed 15:1, although some organizations achieve success with higher ratios. The collection supervisor should have both collections experience and good management skills. Management should require that supervisors regularly review the collectors' performance in areas such as number of contacts made, time per contact, and promises to pay versus dollars received.

The examiner should understand how management determines the optimum level of accounts per collector, a crucial factor in preventing and controlling charge-offs. Surveys of collection departments report that the average number of accounts per collector approximates 300, although this can vary widely depending upon the type of account (bank card or retail) and the technology used. Also, front-end (early delinquency) collectors may handle significantly more than 300 accounts, while back-end (severe delinquency) collectors typically handle less.

Collection strategies determine which accounts collectors actually work, the timing of collection activities, and the manner of the contact (e.g., phone calls, collection letters, and legal letters). In many banks, collection strategies rely on behavioral scoring models which predict the likelihood of collection. Some banks also use champion/challenger collection strategies. Armed with such information, management can effectively direct collection efforts with an emphasis on dollars at risk. Management must maintain close control over collection strategies because, in some cases, a seemingly minor change can significantly impact the dollars collected. The examiner should review the collection strategy process and reports generated, and discuss them with bank management.

Examiners must have a general understanding of the technologies employed by collection departments in order to evaluate their effectiveness. They also should review the collection training program. Nearly all well-managed operations have formal training programs for new employees which include both classroom and on-the-job training.

Management of an account increasingly includes practices such as reaging, fixed payment, and Consumer Credit Counseling Service programs. How management supervises and controls these programs determines the level of risk, if any, they pose to the bank. The following sections provide more information on these areas and others important in the collection process.

Reaging

The credit card industry has an established practice called reaging (also known as curing and rollback). Reaging involves changing the delinquency status of an account. The term applies to both forward and backward changes, and often occurs in both the customer service and collection areas. For example, a payment on an account subsequently returned for non-sufficient funds could result in reaging into a more severe delinquency status, whereas a delinquent account could be brought current if certain payment requirements are met. This discussion, however, will focus on collection reages which bring a delinquent account to a current status.

The practice of bringing a delinquent account current originated to acknowledge and assist customers who corrected previous, usually one-time, cash flow problems. To prevent the accounts from showing perpetually delinquent, the bank would reage them to show current. The practice has continued to grow in recent years, however, and is no longer tied to the recognition of a one-time, nonrecurring problem.

Most banks reage a delinquent account to a current status after receiving three consecutive minimum monthly payments. The underlying philosophy is that three consecutive payments evidence the customer's ongoing capacity and willingness to pay. Some banks' practices differ from this. The examiner should carefully review the analysis that supports the bank's decision to reage accounts and the bank's reaging parameters. The examiner should understand the reaging program in place and review available MIS reports. The examiner should then assess the bank's reaging practices, including management's supervision of the activity.

Because of potential risks associated with reaging, the practice should be governed by appropriate policies and procedures. The bank's reaging policy should address the following:

- Approval and reporting requirements.

- Age of the account before it is eligible for reaging.

- Delinquency levels eligible for reaging.

- Status of the account while reaging: closed, blocked, or open.

- Time limitations between reagings as well as any limitations on the number of reagings permitted for each account.

- Consideration of the borrower's overall capacity to repay (factors such as income, length of employment, and other debts) in the reaging decision.

- Number of payments required to qualify for reaging.

An improperly managed reaging program can lead to pools of problem receivables. It can also understate delinquency and charge-off figures, as well as impede accurate analysis of the allowance for loan and lease losses. Therefore, accurate reports for the reaging program are necessary. At a minimum, management should review regular reports showing both the number and dollar amount of newly reaged accounts (current month) and those reaged within the last 12 months. Management also should monitor cumulative historical data which shows the performance of reaged accounts over time. Without such information, management cannot effectively determine how reaging impacts the bank. For example, if the bank ultimately charges off a large percentage of reaged accounts within a 12-month time frame, management must determine whether the outcome (dollars collected prior to charge off versus collection costs) justifies the practice.

Fixed Payment Programs

Another practice often used in the collection arena is the fixed payment program (also known as cure, zero, or reduced-interest programs). Such workout programs are targeted to borrowers with prolonged or severe credit problems in an attempt to both work with the borrower and to encourage continued repayment.

While most banks offer one or more fixed payment/workout programs, program characteristics vary greatly within the industry. Programs typically consist of a fixed payment amount, a lower minimum payment percentage, and/or a reduced interest rate for a specified period of time (usually 12 months). As an additional incentive, banks generally reage the accounts to current upon receipt of a specified number of consecutive payments at the newly agreed upon rate/amount.

Loss rates associated with fixed payment programs are generally higher than those of the total portfolio because of the borrowers' financial problems. The bank should have policies that specify the terms and conditions of fixed payment programs, such as qualifications for entering the program and how long an account can stay in the program. Management should institute strong controls and ongoing monitoring and perform regular analyses of the programs to determine whether they ultimately benefit or harm the bank.

The examiner should assess the prudence of the fixed payment programs in place and the dollars involved. Programs which involve excessive amortization periods should be discouraged. The examiner should review management's program analyses and ensure that new programs and/or program modifications are sufficiently substantiated.

Consumer Credit Counseling Service

As part of their collection efforts, many banks also work with the Consumer Credit Counseling Service (CCCS). The CCCS is a nonprofit organization which functions as an independent third party to help consumers work through their financial difficulties. Properly managed, CCCS programs aid both the consumer and the credit community by returning significant funds to the system.

A consumer's acceptance into the CCCS program is based upon a CCCS counselor's determination that his or her financial situation is salvageable. If accepted, the consumer must agree to cancel all credit cards, develop and adhere to a budget (with counselor guidance), and make debt payments as agreed. CCCS then notifies creditors that the consumer has been accepted into the program and negotiates reduced payment terms with each creditor. Terms vary by creditor, with some requiring the full payment amount and others reducing interest and principal payments significantly in an attempt to stop the account from going to loss. Consumers then make their payments directly to CCCS, which pays the creditors.
Upon receiving confirmation of a consumer's acceptance into the program, creditors will normally reage the account to a current status if it is delinquent. At this point the creditor generally waives any late and overlimit fees, and ceases all collection efforts as long as the account complies with the renegotiated terms. If an account goes delinquent again for any significant period of time, it usually reverts to the original contract terms, collection efforts commence, and it is dropped from the CCCS program.

Banks should have a policy regarding CCCS accounts and appropriate systems to properly account for related transactions with the CCCS. Banks typically assign an individual to supervise and monitor its CCCS accounts. The individual should ensure that all CCCS accounts are properly identified to enable accurate reporting of CCCS delinquencies and charge-offs. The bank should incorporate CCCS information into the appropriate loan risk grades and into allowance for loan and lease loss calculations.

MIS for Collections

The collections area generates many MIS reports to help manage the risks associated with this activity. Indeed, regular MIS reports for each collection program are an important aid in proper supervision. Executive management should regularly review key MIS collection reports. Management must be able to identify and quantify all collection program specifics, such as the number of reagings on an account. It should track the performance of each collection program against the performance of the credit card portfolio as a whole. If a program is not working effectively, management must take steps to discontinue or modify it. The examiner should evaluate these executive reports for pertinent information and accuracy and should strongly criticize the absence of necessary MIS reports.

One report, called the rollover, breakage, or roll-rate report, is particularly important. Through this report, management can review the number and dollar volume of accounts that move from current to 30-days delinquent, 30- to 60-days, etc. This information allows management to accurately predict the charge-off rate as far as six months into the future. In addition, this report can aid management decisions regarding collection staffing levels.

Delinquency and charge-off reports serve as valuable tools in evaluating collection effectiveness. Management should review these reports for the gross portfolio as well as on a program-by-program basis. Many credit card operations report delinquencies using two formats, end-of-month (EOM) and sum-of-cycle (SOC). EOM delinquencies are used for call report purposes and reflect outstanding delinquencies at month-end as a percentage of outstanding receivables.

SOC reports compute delinquencies for each billing cycle, then aggregate these cycles to determine delinquency for the total portfolio. Unlike EOM reports, the SOC reports ignore the "cleaning up" of delinquencies between the end of the cycle date and the end of the month.

Management may find reports that analyze delinquencies and charge-offs on a "lagged" basis useful, especially if a portfolio has experienced significant growth. Such analyses take current delinquency and charge-off figures as a percentage of receivables outstanding six or 12 months prior. Also, a "block" or "status code" report provides valuable information for reviewing the composition of the portfolio; i.e., the number and dollar amounts of fixed payment, bankruptcy, fraud, deceased, and canceled accounts. As discussed previously, reaging reports are imperative. Other reports could include actual versus budgeted performance, changes in collection strategies, and performance of behavioral or other scoring models.

Delinquency, Classification, and Charge-off Policies

Bank management should regularly review the quality of the portfolio through a variety of means including past due, charge-off, and profitability reports. Management's ability to quickly identify trends in the portfolio and to react appropriately is a critical element in proper and consistent credit card management. In banks lacking a timely charge-off program, loss ratios may be meaningless for periods of less than one year. As a result, management may not become aware of downward trends until year-end or until examiners initiate charge-offs. This delays recognition of problems as well as the implementation of necessary corrective action.

The examiner should determine how management charges off contractual and noncontractual losses such as bankruptcy, fraud, and deceased accounts. If the bank charges off delinquent credit card loans in the normal course of business, under a policy consistent with regulatory guidelines, examiners usually should not need to request charge-offs during the examination.

The following policy is restated from the *Comptroller's Handbook* section on Credit Card Plans, dated March 1990:

Review should be limited to ascertaining that exceptions meet established guidelines. If the bank is properly charging off delinquent credit card loans in the normal course of business, under a policy which generally conforms to that of the Office of the Comptroller of the Currency (OCC), no specific request for charge-off should be necessary. Credit card accounts delinquent four to six zero billing cycles will be classified substandard and accounts delinquent seven zero billing cycles will be classified loss. In order to ensure uniform interpretation of the phrase "delinquent seven zero billings," the following definition and example is provided:

The examiner should ascertain the payment terms of the contracts to determine the grace period. In keeping with the present OCC policy on monthly payment contracts, which are not considered delinquent until 30 days after the due date, allowance for the grace period must be made in order to determine the due date. A bank credit card customer generally has 25 days in which to pay billings before the loan is considered delinquent. If no payment is made between two billing cycles, the balance is considered five days delinquent. If no payment is received before issuance of still another statement, the balance is technically 35-days delinquent. However, current practice is to define accounts with two zero billings as 30-days delinquent.

Reference is made to the example, shown below, and the word "delinquent" is stressed. The example assumes a 30-day billing cycle and that the cardholder has 25 days (the most common term) to either pay the contract in full or make the agreed partial payment with service charge. In view of this, the first billing cannot be construed as a delinquent billing.

Since the cardholder has a grace period to make the payment, the phrase "delinquent seven zero billings" means, in effect, those contracts that have had no full payments by the cardholder for a cumulative total of seven billings. This policy does not preclude the classification of assets delinquent for a lesser period when classification is warranted.

Example

Billing number	Zero billings	Cumulative days delinquent*	Comments
1	0	0	
2	1	5	
3	2	30	OCC considers delinquent
4	3	60	
5	4	90	Substandard
6	5	120	Substandard
7	6	150	Substandard
8	7	180	Loss

* A payment equivalent to 90 percent or more of the contractual payment may be considered a full payment in computing delinquency.

Some credit card operations have "forgiveness" programs which are used to eliminate insignificant, small delinquencies. Typically automated, they forgive a small portion of the delinquent payment. This forgiveness can take the form of either a percentage of the minimum payment due or a specific dollar amount. Forgiveness programs should comply with the FFIEC's guidelines for partial payments.

In addition to the delinquency charge-off policy, the examiner should ensure that the bank charges off bankruptcy, fraud, and deceased accounts in a timely manner. The same charge-off policy, identified above, would apply unless the loss is identified earlier. In most instances, permitting them to age through the delinquency categories to charge off may not be acceptable. Losses from bankruptcy, fraud, and deceased accounts should be charged off when the loss is determined.

In the case of fraudulent accounts, the bank should place a block on the account until it can complete its fraud investigation. Once the bank verifies fraud, FFIEC Instructions for the Reports of Condition and Income direct the balance be charged against miscellaneous expense (versus the allowance).

Recoveries

Recoveries represent collection activities conducted after the charge-off of an account. The rate of recovery depends on many factors including:

- Charge-off policy in place.

- Previous collection efforts.

- Depth and experience of staff.

- Adequacy of systems and controls.

- Use of technology.

Recovery activities are generally conducted internally and then out-placed to collection agencies after several months. When out-placing accounts, the bank must maintain strict controls and appropriate systems to evaluate each agency's performance. Collection agencies receive a percentage of the dollars collected, typically between 30 percent and 60 percent. The amount varies based on whether the agency is the primary (the first agency to work the accounts), secondary, or tertiary collector. Fees are lowest for the primary agency (these are the accounts easiest to collect) and highest for the tertiary agency. The bank should periodically rotate out-placed accounts between agencies to ensure they are actively and appropriately worked.

Fraud Control

Fraud is a continuing problem associated with credit card programs. The very nature of the product, an easily obtainable unsecured line of credit that is basically managed by the consumer, makes it an ideal mechanism for fraud. The bank card associations, issuers and acquirers, the U.S. Postal Service, and other vendors have been focusing on strengthening systems and controls to reduce fraudulent activities. Because of the advances in fraud detection, fraud losses, measured as a percent of sales volume, have declined during the past several years for many issuers.

Management should have appropriate systems and controls in place to control fraud losses. The proper training of employees regarding fraud systems and controls, fraud recognition and handling, and accurate MIS reporting is critical in maintaining fraud losses at or below industry averages.

Fraud can be orchestrated in many ways. Lost/stolen cards and non-receipt of issued cards represent a large percentage of all fraud reported. The bank card associations track fraud according to type and most issuers follow this or a similar format in reporting fraud in their internal MIS reports. Reporting specific information on types of fraud allows a bank to better identify its points of greatest risk. If the operation does not distinguish fraud losses by type, the examiner should discuss the benefits of such reporting with bank management.

Issuers should review their average fraud losses to determine if the staff is identifying fraud activities in a timely manner. If the issuer has inadequate systems and controls to identify fraud, this will likely result in frauds running longer, permitting more transactions, and eventually higher losses.

Card issuers recently have pursued some of the following activities to reduce fraud:

- Sorting mail outside of the facility where the mail was initiated.

- Instituting call-to-activate (CTA) requirements for new cards and reissued cards.

- Implementing pattern recognition programs and systems.

- Developing neural networks/expert systems. (See Appendix A for more detail on neural networks.)

- Extending the time in which cards are reissued to three years from two years to reduce the number of cards in the delivery system.

- Designating a special group to handle lost/stolen card reports.

- Increasing the level of payment review to include all checks over a certain amount, $3,000 for example, regardless of whether or not there is a payment coupon.

Most large issuers maintain dedicated fraud staffs that supervise the many activities required when a card holder notifies the issuer or the issuer becomes aware of a fraud. These activities include:

- Preparing a lost/stolen report from the card holder and advising the card holder to destroy additional cards. The report may include: account number, name, fraud type, address, city, state, zip, number of transactions, dollar amount of fraud, charge-off month, date, description of fraudulent activity, corrective action taken, if any, name of preparer, name of manager signing off.

- Blocking the account and placing it on an exception file. Each issuer will have its own block codes depending upon its processor.

- Preparing a request to issue new cards to the cardholder. This includes reviewing activity in the blocked account and transferring legitimate transactions to a replacement account. Fraudulent transactions are retained on the old account.

- Setting up a file for investigation on fraud accounts. This includes requesting draft copies of fraudulent items and challenging the card holder on questionable items.

- Reviewing and initiating fraud transactions for chargebacks. This includes preparing fraud notifications to Visa/MasterCard, investigating and documenting fraud cards, and prosecuting, if possible.

- Charging off losses after a certain number of months of activity or closure of the investigation. The issuer subsequently submits losses to Visa/MasterCard for reimbursement on insurance.

Issuers should have adequate systems and controls in place to ensure that fraudulent activities are recognized in a timely manner and the accounts are appropriately blocked to prevent future authorizations. The timing of the block date is important as the vast majority of fraud losses occur on or prior to the block date and those after the block date have significantly lower transaction sizes. According to industry studies, improvement in authorization and other fraud control measures has materially lowered losses from fraud after the block date.

Fraud accounts are typically reaged at the time of notification and/or identification to permit the investigation to proceed without reaching the mandatory charge-off period of 180 days contractual delinquency. Many operations charge off fraud losses within 30 days of the completed investigation. The investigation period normally does not exceed 90 days. This period provides the fraud unit with ample time to conduct its investigation. Times significantly in excess of this period should be discussed with management. Fraud losses are taken against miscellaneous expense.

Allowance for Loan Losses

The methods used to establish and maintain the allowance for loan losses in credit card portfolios will vary among banks. The examiner must review the bank's method to determine if it is reasonable and adequately documented for that bank's particular circumstances. The examiner must recognize that no method can determine the appropriate reserve level with absolute precision; instead, reasonable estimates must be made based upon careful analysis of the portfolio.

Examiners must determine whether the bank's method adequately identifies the inherent loss in the portfolio. An inherent loss is an unconfirmed loss that probably exists based on information available when the evaluation is made. The amount of the loss must be subject to reasonable estimation. Losses in large, relatively homogeneous portfolios such as credit card portfolios are generally easier to estimate than other portfolios. (See the Comptroller's booklet entitled *Allowance for Loan and Lease Losses* for a discussion of inherent loss and other concepts.)

A common estimation of a reserve's adequacy is the aggregate level of portfolio turnover. Credit card loss reserves are generally maintained for outstanding loans rather than committed lines. By their nature, the life cycle of a given level of credit card outstandings is relatively short on a portfolio basis. Typically, portfolios repay, or "turn" in less than 12 months, as measured by either credit card "sales" or payments.

Measured by the aggregate approach, a reserve level less than the anticipated losses for the portfolio turnover period may not be adequate. For example, if a bank's analysis shows that the portfolio "turns" every six months, a loss reserve representing significantly less than a corresponding six months of forecast losses may not be adequate. Conversely, reserves in excess of the portfolio turnover period might be overstated by, in effect, representing reserves for outstanding loans not yet on the books.

Portfolio turnover is only a reasonable estimation of a reserve's adequacy. Management and examiners also should consider other factors in assessing reserve adequacy; such as current and previous underwriting standards, marketing, delinquencies and age of accounts, bankruptcy and charge-off trends; collection practices, including reaging and concessionary payment activity; the bank's charge-off policy; projected portfolio growth; the financial condition and support of companies associated with significant corporate card and private label programs; concentrations; and changes in portfolio mix.

Reserving for Rebate Programs

Over recent years, competition within the credit card industry has required issuers to become increasingly aggressive in account acquisition. The emergence of nonbank card issuers, CEBA credit card banks, (see glossary) and cobranding partners has intensified the marketing thrust to the consumer. Many issuers, either directly or through a partnership arrangement, offer some type of rebate program to cardholders. Rebates may be cash, free gas, free phone time, free airline tickets, monies toward car purchases, and any number of other items.

The cobranding partnership contract is very important to determine the issuer's costs, marketing requirements, and liabilities, if any. In most arrangements, the partner has the contingent liability based upon a rebate formula involving card holder purchase dollar sales volume. In some cases, however, the contract could be negotiated to give the issuer some of the contingent liability on the rebate program. The bank should factor contract terms, particularly covering liability, into pricing the partnership relationship. If the issuer has contingent liability, it should reserve for the liability as described below.

Increasingly, issuers are marketing proprietary card products which contain rebate features. In these cases, the contingent liability pertaining to the rebate redemption rests with the issuer. Because of this, the issuer must reserve for this future redemption liability and the examiner must make a judgment as to the rebate reserve's adequacy and to the reasonableness of the reserve method.

If the issuer has contingent liability on any rebate program, the examiner should approach the analysis similar to evaluating the adequacy of the allowance for loan losses. The issuer should have an accounting policy which governs the rebate reserve method. If no such policy is in place, the examiner should discuss the need for a policy with management. The policy should address issues such as:

- Under what general ledger account the reserve will be located.

- Under what account the expense will be located.

- How monthly accruals will be determined.

- What subsidiary ledgers must be maintained.

- How often the analysis must be prepared.

- What level of management must attest to the adequacy of the reserve.

- What level of management approval is required to change the reserve method.

- How redemptions will be handled.

- How over and under reserve levels will be handled.

- How data bases will interface or how data will be exchanged regarding point accounting, redemption transactions, etc., if outside vendors are used in the redemption process.

In conducting the analysis of the adequacy of a rebate reserve, the examiner should review the method and determine how long the program has been in existence and if it has undergone any significant modifications regarding rebates and/or rebate reserve methods. The type of product the issuer or retailer is promoting will have a material impact on the type of reserve method that management will use. For example, the rebate reserve method for a program that provides for a card holder to accumulate points toward the purchase of airline tickets will be different from a program that annually rebates 1 percent of net purchase sales back to the account holder in cash. Many programs have rebate limitations during specific time periods. If no limitations are apparent, the examiner should discuss with management and try to evaluate what, if any, risk this poses to the issuer's financial statements.

Outside vendors may be used to provide a variety of services for rebate programs, including accounting and redemption. Examiners should assess who is involved in the rebate operation, how information is passed between systems, and how payments are transacted.

Profit Analysis

Credit card operations have traditionally offered banks substantial opportunities for profit. An issuing bank's credit card operation commonly generates two to three times the return on assets of other product lines. Profit margins on credit card accounts can be deceptive, however, and thorough analyses of the credit card operation's financial statements are necessary to draw accurate conclusions. Moreover, the profitability of the credit card area is not static. It is influenced by cyclical trends in the consumer retail area and in the economy in general.

Any profitability analysis must start with a review of the credit card operation's strategic plan. Strategic goals can be very different among issuers. For instance, credit card operations owned by retailers may be concerned primarily with increasing incremental sales of the retailer. They may lower their credit standards to put more of the retailer's cards in circulation. While this increases sales for the retailer, it may reduce profitability of the credit card operation because it could lead to higher credit losses.

The credit card operation should have a system to measure overall profitability, including direct and indirect costs. The operation should have detailed budgets that are compared, on a monthly basis, against actual results with significant variances investigated. The bank periodically should perform "what if" scenarios that estimate the impact of economic changes, competition, and legislative issues on the portfolio. Lastly, management should prepare pro forma financial statements on major new product roll outs and/or modification of significant terms on existing product lines to identify potential effects on income streams.

The credit card operation should prepare profit analyses for the total portfolio and each individual portfolio or program. Also, it is increasingly necessary for the operation to manage profit levels at the individual account level. A limited number of card operations currently have the systems in place to focus down to this level. As profit margins continue to narrow and account retention becomes increasingly important, more credit card operations are likely to have individual account level systems in place. Such a system provides management with the data to help it focus retention efforts by determining such things as accounts on which to waive annual membership fees.

Most major issuers have separate and distinct finance areas to supervise the accounting of income and expenses. These areas should have in place appropriate MIS reports that, at a minimum, detail income and expense for executive management summary reports. Good management information systems are crucial in ensuring that management has an accurate profitability picture. The finance area generally is responsible for coordinating and preparing the budget and strategic goals as well as generating any reports to the parent company, Visa/MasterCard, and regulatory agencies.

Profitability among credit card operations may vary widely based upon a number of factors such as management competence, risk appetite, products offered, affinity/cobranding relationships, and the method used to report various costs. Management must have strong accounting and reporting systems in place to supervise the business effectively. (See Appendix C for examples of ways to examine the profitability of credit card operations.)

There are several common measures of the overall profitability of a credit card portfolio. These include return on average assets (ROA), return on equity (ROE), and income per billed account. ROE measures help determine the market's perception of the bank's financial performance. They can, however, vary significantly depending upon securitization volumes and capital leverage. Consequently, their use to gauge financial performance for credit card operations should be scrutinized closely.

Profitability analyses of credit card operations should always be conducted on a managed portfolio basis instead of a booked asset basis (net of securitized assets). This is important for banks that remove receivables from the balance sheet through securitization or participations structured like a securitization transaction. In such transactions, receivables are taken off the balance sheet while a residual income stream generated from these receivables continues to flow to the bank. Therefore, if profitability analyses only look to booked receivables, the traditional operating performance of the portfolio will be overstated.

The examiner must know the sources of income and expense to analyze the profitability of a credit card operation. Some of the basic components of income in a credit card operation are finance charges, annual and service fees, and interchange fees. Some credit card operations receive servicing fees and residual income from securitized portfolios.

Finance charges are the primary revenue source and represent interest assessed against revolving balances. Interest rates vary widely depending upon products, borrowers' risk profiles, competition, and state usury laws.

The annual and service fee component of income includes fees assessed to the customer for use of the card. Annual fees vary and are generally tailored to the perceived value of the card and associated enhancements, such as travel insurance or check cashing privileges. Service fees are transaction fees imposed on certain transactions such as cash advances, late payments, and overlines. Interchange fees represent a fee to the issuer that is extracted from the discount fee paid by a merchant who accepts a credit card transaction.

Some basic components of expense include account acquisition and credit processing costs, card issuing, authorizations, collections, loan loss provisions, card holder servicing and promotion, card holder billing, payment processing, and fraud investigations. Another possible expense item may be payments to affinity and cobranding partners.

Overhead expenses tend to be higher in credit card operations than in other areas of a bank. The small size of individual accounts and the high transactional volume create higher costs per account. Because in-house data processing costs are expensive, many operations chose to contract their processing to third-party processors.

Cost of funds is a major expense item, making up nearly half of an issuer's total expense distribution, and varies depending on the funding sources used by the bank. A bank's cost of funds also will depend upon its condition and reputation in the market. Many large credit card issuers use securitization as a source of funding. The examiner should discuss trends in funding costs and composition with the bank and investigate unusual variances.

In reviewing income and expense categories, it is helpful to compare the bank's performance against peer averages. The examiner should inquire whether the bank has recent industry cost studies. The bank card associations periodically provide their members with cost studies and other industry data.

Securitized Assets

The securitization of receivables is an important funding vehicle for some credit card issuers. Securitization is the pooling of assets with similar characteristics into a standard format for sale to investors. With regard to credit cards, the issuer sells receivables (not the accounts) to a trust while retaining an interest in a portion of the pool. Certificates representing the vast majority of the pool, usually 80 percent to 90 percent, are then sold to investors as asset-backed securities (ABS).

Asset securitization can offer the following advantages:

- Provide an alternative source of funding.

- Remove assets from the balance sheet for assets sold without recourse, which improves capital ratios and certain performance ratios and possibly reduces reserve requirements.

- Reduce exposures to credit and interest rate risk.

- Improve the liquidity and marketability of the securitized assets.

- Allow the bank to receive regular servicing, residual (excess servicing), and other fee income.

To attract investors, securitized transactions typically must be supported by credit enhancements that protect the investor if portfolio performance fails to meet predetermined levels. Appropriate enhancements allow the security to obtain a "AAA" rating at origination. The exception is securities with a senior/subordinate structure, in which the subordinate portion usually has a lower rating, unless it is heavily enhanced. Credit enhancements can include a spread account, letter of credit, cash collateral account, or subordination agreement. (See the glossary for definitions of these terms.)

The credit enhancement for a securitization primarily provides protection for the investors, but also normally gives the examiner information about the market's view of the bank's credit card operations. An overall increase in the amount of credit enhancement needed to bring a securitization to market may indicate that the market perceives some weakness in underwriting, collections, fraud control, or servicing capabilities. Credit enhancement is most often in the form of subordinated classes of securities, supplemented with cash collateral and spread accounts. To assess market perception, the examiner may compare the relative amount of credit enhancement that was necessary to get a "AAA" rating for the most senior piece of a multi-level securitized transaction, with past securitized issuances by the same bank and other issuers' current deals.

ABS are usually structured to pay interest only during a revolving period, followed by an amortization period. During the revolving period, the investors' principal portion remains at a fixed level. The originator's (issuing bank) interest in the pool fluctuates since it serves as a buffer to keep the investor portion at a fixed level. All principal payments from card holders are paid from the trust to the originator and are used to purchase additional receivables. Revolving periods usually last two to seven years.

During the amortization period, cash flows received from customers are paid to investors and the originator based on their pro rata ownership interests. When the investors' principal portion is fully paid, the originator owns 100 percent of the receivables in the trust. Some ABS have bullet amortization structures which make a single principal payment on the maturity date. Banks that use securitization as a source of funding for their credit card originations often repackage the receivables at maturity for a new securitized issuance.

Most revolving credit card Master Trusts (see below) contain early amortization triggers. These triggers are in place to protect the investor should the portfolio not perform at certain predetermined levels. Generally, triggers are tied to maintenance of a predetermined portfolio yield and loss rate. If a trigger is activated, the trust must begin early amortization of the security. Each series within a Master Trust may have its own specific trigger, which should be tracked by the bank's MIS reports. Depending upon the structure of the trust, individual series may go into early amortization without affecting the Master Trust.

The unexpected funding needs associated with an early amortization event can pose liquidity concerns for the originating bank. The triggering of an early amortization event results in the trust immediately passing principal payments through to investors. This leaves the bank, as owner of the underlying accounts, responsible for funding new charges that would normally have been purchased by the trust. Banks should have liquidity contingency plans which address this potential unexpected funding requirement. Management should receive and review MIS reports showing the performance of the securitized portfolio in relation to the early amortization triggers.

Many large credit card issuers began securitizing receivables under a Master Trust structure in 1988. In a Master Trust structure, several issues or series share the rights to a common pool of receivables. As long as certain conditions are satisfied, a bank can issue multiple series out of the same Master Trust, simultaneously or over a period of time.

Series in the same Master Trust can have different cash flow structures, maturities, early amortization events, credit enhancement levels, ratings, and principal repayment mechanisms. Some structures also provide for a Master Trust to be subdivided into groups of series to interconnect some series, or to limit the effect of some series to that group.

Unlike the stand-alone trust structure in which receivables from selected accounts are assigned for the life of the trust, most Master Trust agreements allow card-issuing banks to assign additional receivables to the trust. In addition to adding receivables when a bank issues a new series, a bank may add receivables to replace those balances lost to card holder attrition or maintain the characteristics of the existing pool. Some Master Trust agreements permit limited lump sum additions without notifying the ratings agencies. An issuer also may be required to add or remove receivables to maintain a minimum prescribed level.

The bank should have comprehensive policies and procedures addressing asset securitization. These policies should address required approvals, selection of assets, and initial and ongoing reporting requirements. Bank management should periodically report to the board of directors on the performance of securitized assets.

The bank also should have a plan for servicing securitized assets. The examiner should determine whether the bank's current systems, including staffing, are capable of handling the requirements for the current and anticipated securitization volume. The bank's failure to adequately service the portfolio could trigger an early amortization event.

Bank MIS should provide a summary of initial terms and ongoing performance of its securitizations. The examiner should review the terms of each securitization and analyze associated risks, focusing on the pricing and credit enhancements of the securitization. For example, a securitization with a fixed coupon payment exposes the bank to future interest rate risk, but allows management to plan its cash flows with certainty. Conversely, a securitization with a floating rate coupon means that the bank limits appreciable interest rate risk, but is potentially exposed to future liquidity risk.

Income Analysis for Securitized Assets

Securitization changes the composition of the institution's income. On a nominal basis, the result is less interest income and more fee-based income. Examiners must realize, however, that securitization does not change the true operating performance of the retail lending portfolio.

Securitizations must be included in any review of the portfolio's earnings and asset quality. For example, prior to the securitization, a bank's portfolio might show a 2 percent pre-tax return on assets. After securitization, when the return is calculated on the new, smaller asset figure, it appears higher (for example, it might move from 2 percent to 5 percent). The dollar income generated, however, remains unchanged. An assessment based on the portfolio net of securitized assets is an inaccurate indicator of performance. A more appropriate way to analyze return would be to look at the performance of all assets under management.

Reviews of asset quality and collection efforts, including reaging and fixed payment programs, should include the securitized portfolio. Aggressive reaging or other collection programs could understate delinquency rates and charge-offs, and misrepresent the portfolio's performance to the investors.
Buying back problem loans may constitute recourse on the transaction for the issuer/originator. Under current regulatory accounting procedure, recourse transactions are accounted for as financings rather than sales, placing more stress on the bank's capital structure.

Generally accepted accounting procedure (GAAP) currently prescribes a different reporting treatment than regulatory accounting procedure (RAP) for securitization profit. Under RAP, an issuer may not book profits for securitizations at origination by applying present value standards to the expected income from the spread account, a treatment acceptable under GAAP. RAP treatment does not allow a bank to report as income monthly payments to the spread account that exceed the cost of servicing until investor claims are extinguished. On the other hand, under GAAP, the bank may report any excess service fees as income over the life of the security.

On January 1, 1997, RAP will conform with GAAP on securitization profits. Until that time, the examiner should analyze the effects of these GAAP/RAP differences on current and future RAP earnings. More information on GAAP and RAP accounting can be found in Financial Accounting Standard (FAS) 77 (changes to FAS 125 on January 1, 1997) and the Instructions to the Consolidated Reports of Condition and Income issued by the FFIEC.

Purchased Credit Card Relationships

Purchased credit card relationships (PCCRs) are intangible assets that are created when a bank acquires a credit card portfolio at a premium from a third party. Generally, Visa/MasterCard portfolios are purchased at a premium, usually 10 percent to 25 percent over outstanding receivables; the amount over the par value (the premium) of the portfolio is the PCCR. The cost of acquiring a private label portfolio varies widely and may even be made at a discount. Management may elect to divide the PCCR into different categories, such as non-compete, loan loss, yield adjustment, and goodwill. The purchase price can be determined by a variety of factors that, in aggregate, drive the cash flows of the portfolio. Some of the main factors considered are the yield, attrition rates, charge-off rates, funding rates, and processing costs.

Most credit card portfolio purchasers maintain automated software models that management can load with its best estimates of how the proposed portfolio will perform. This data is obtained from the brokers and/or sellers and will be used to determine the initial bid on the portfolio. If the bank is selected to perform a due diligence exam (because it offered one of the highest bids) it will then modify the model with enhanced data obtained from the due diligence exam. The model will generally create cash flow data, income statements, balance sheets, equity flows, etc. that will permit the purchaser to determine an appropriate value to place on the portfolio, usually based upon an internal earnings hurdle rate. Models typically used include discount cash flow models, discounted capital flow models, and return on asset models. (See Appendix E for a detailed discussion of how to analyze purchased credit card relationships.)

Glossary

Acquirer, acquiring member, or merchant bank. A bank, financial institution, or other MasterCard or Visa member that maintains the merchant relationship and receives all credit card transactions; sometimes referred to as the acquiring bank.

Affinity card. A credit card issued by a bank in conjunction with an organization or collective group; for example, profession, alumni, retired persons association. The card issuer often pays the sponsoring organization a fee.

Agent bank. A bank that, by agreement, participates in another bank's card program, usually by turning over its applicants for bank cards to the bank administering the card program and by acting as a depository for merchants.

Cash collateral account. This is a credit enhancement common in asset-backed security structures. The cash collateral account is held in a segregated trust account, funded at the outset of the deal, and can be drawn on to cover shortfalls in interest, principal, or servicing expense for a particular series if the excess spread is reduced to zero.

CEBA bank. This is a special kind of issuing bank. The term CEBA bank comes from enactment of the Competitive Equality Banking Act of 1987 (CEBA), which established conditions for special-purpose credit card banks. CEBA banks may only accept time and savings deposits of $100,000 or more. They typically have a nonbank holding company parent. They are often affiliated with a retailer and offer private label cards for use at the affiliated organization. They may, however, issue a general purpose Visa or MasterCard instead.

Champion/challenger strategy. Management applies one strategy against a portion of the portfolio (champion) and other strategies (challengers) against additional segments of the portfolio to identify a more successful practice.

Chargeback. A dispute procedure initiated by the card issuer after receipt of the initial presentment from the acquirer. The issuer may determine that, for a given reason, the transaction was presented in violation of the rules or procedures and is eligible to be returned to the acquirer for possible remedy.

Cobranded card. A card issued by a bank bearing the logo and name of another company that has a commercial purpose. There is usually some type of rebate or added benefit for the consumer.

Convenience user. A card holder who pays the balance in full on each payment due date.

Corporate card. A card issued to companies for use by company employees. The liability for abuse of the card typically rests with the company and not with the employee.

Credit card. A plastic card used to purchase goods and services and to obtain cash advances on credit, for which the card holder is subsequently billed by the issuing institution for repayment of the credit extended.

Credit scoring. A statistical method for predicting the creditworthiness of credit applicants.

Independent sales organization (ISO). An outside company contracted by banks to administer merchant and/or card holder servicing.

Interchange rate. The fee extracted from the discount fee paid by the merchant who accepted the credit card transaction. Interchange fees are set by the bank card associations (MasterCard and Visa) based upon the size and method of transmission from the merchant.

Issuer. The institution (or its agent) that issues the card to the cardholder, sometimes, referred to as the issuing bank.

Letter of credit (LC). This is a type of guarantee provided by a third party. On most securitizations, the LC is a second layer of enhancement, after a spread account. LCs are less attractive enhancements because they depend on the financial standing of the issuing bank. If that bank is downgraded by the ratings agencies, the securitized issue also is likely to be downgraded.

Merchant authorization. The means of receiving sales validation for the merchant, by telephone or authorization terminal, to guarantee payment to the merchant.

Periodic rate. An amount of finance charge expressed as a percentage that is to be applied to a credit card loan balance for a specified period, usually monthly.

Point-of-sale (POS). The location where a customer makes a purchase from a merchant.

Reaging (also curing or rollback). The practice of bringing a delinquent account current.

Rollover. The practice of carrying forward a portion of an outstanding balance on a cardholder's account from month-to-month.

Securitization. The process of creating an investment security backed by credit card receivables.

Settlement. The process by which acquirers and issuers exchange financial data and value resulting from sales transactions, cash advances, merchandise credits, etc.

Spread account. This is the most common form of a securitization credit enhancement. It is a reserve account that absorbs credit losses. The spread account generally equals two to three times the expected losses in the package of receivables. This spread account is initially "seeded" (funded) by the selling bank. These advances are usually expensed to achieve regulatory accounting procedure (RAP) sale treatment. Excess servicing income is deposited into this account each month until it is fully funded and the seed money is repaid to the selling bank. The account is controlled by the trustee.

Subordination agreement. This is another securitization credit enhancement arrangement that identifies senior and subordinated portions of the security issue. The enhancement is to the senior portion, which gains payment priority in terms of amortization and in the event of liquidation.

Third-party processing. The processing of transactions by parties acting under contract to card issuers or acquirers.

Vintage. The year of origin of a cardholder's account.

General Procedures

Objective: Determine the scope of the credit card lending examination.

1. Review the following to identify if previous problems require follow-up. Determine if planned corrective action was effected; and, if not, why not.

   ☐ Previous ROE.
   ☐ Supervisory strategy and other supervisory comments in the OCC's electronic information systems.
   ☐ EIC's scope memorandum.
   ☐ Bank management's response to previous examination findings.
   ☐ Audit reports, and working papers, if necessary.
   ☐ Bank correspondence on credit card lending.

2. From the EIC or appropriate examining personnel, obtain the results the analysis of the UBPR, BERT, and other OCC reports. Identify any concerns, trends, or changes involving credit card lending since the last examination.

3. In addition to the general information requested in the LPM program, obtain and review any other internal reports management uses to supervise credit card lending activities. Examples include:

   ☐ The credit card strategic or business plan.
   ☐ Executive management summary reports for credit cards.
   ☐ Credit card loan policies and procedures.
   ☐ An organization chart including each functional area.
   ☐ Copies of formal job descriptions for all principal positions.
   ☐ Resumes of principals in the department.
   ☐ Copies of credit card compensation programs or incentive plans.
   ☐ Copies of any reports provided to the board of directors concerning credit card operations since the last examination.
   ☐ Copies of all internal and external audit reports covering the credit card operations since the last examination, with any management responses.
   ☐ A list of board and executive or senior management committees, which supervise the credit card operation, including a list of members and meeting schedules. Also, obtain copies of minutes documenting those meetings since the last examination.
   ☐ The beginning of the year credit card budget and any revisions as of the examination date.
   ☐ A summary of all credit card products offered and a brief description of their characteristics, including pricing.
   ☐ Copies of Visa, MasterCard, or other applicable association standards and copies of all correspondence from these organizations since the last examination.
   ☐ Copies of credit card marketing plans, overall and by product.
   ☐ A list of scoring models used and copies of manuals. Obtain a list of credit bureaus used and the scoring models they employ.
   ☐ A list of the bank's affinity affiliations and copies of cobranding contracts.
   ☐ A list of any credit card concentrations of credit.
   ☐ Copies of any credit card loan review reports since last examination.

☐ A balance sheet and income and expense statement for the credit card operation as of the examination date and most recent year-end.

☐ A list of credit card portfolios acquired since the last examination, including terms of the purchase, and copies of any due diligence reports relating to those acquisitions.

☐ If applicable, a list of credit card securitizations and copies of each prospectus associated with those offerings.

When requested information is received, verify its completeness with the request list.

4.   Determine, during early discussions with management:

- How they supervise the credit card department.
- If there have been any significant changes in policies, practices, or personnel, since the last examination.
- If there are any internal or external factors that could affect credit card lending.

5.   Determine the scope of this examination based on findings from the steps above and discussions with the bank EIC and other appropriate supervisors. Set examination objectives.

6.   In consultation with the EIC, determine which of the following credit card related areas will be examined in detail. Refer to the specific procedures for these areas in the Quantity and Quality of risk sections, to perform the steps necessary to meet your examination objectives.

- Scoring Models.
- Marketing.
- New Accounts.
    - Preapproved Account Solicitations.
    - Application-based Account Acquisitions and Underwriting.
    - Portfolio Acquisitions and Underwriting.
- Types of Credit Cards.
    - Affinity and Cobranding Programs.
    - Corporate Card Programs.
    - Secured Credit Card Programs.
    - Private Label Card Programs.
- Account Management.
- Collections.
- Securitized Assets.
- Purchased Credit Card Relationships (PCCR).
- Allowance for Loan and Lease Losses.
- Miscellaneous Credit Card Procedures.
    - Management and Organization.
    - Risk Management.
    - Profit Analysis.
    - Concentrations.
    - Compliance with Laws and Regulations.

Note: Select from among the following examination procedures those steps that are necessary to meet your objective. All steps are seldom required in all examinations.

Quantity of Risk

Conclusion: The quantity of risk is (low, moderate, or high).

Objective: To assess the quantity of risk associated with the bank's credit card lending operations.

General

1. Review the most recent executive management summary reports for the credit card operation and identify any material changes in types of products offered and/or market focus, underwriting criteria, volumes, and trends.

2. Review credit card policies and identify any significant changes since the last examination.

Scoring Models

1. Evaluate the bank's scoring models and documentation supporting the models. Determine:

    - That the developer warrants that the scoring models are empirically derived and statistically sound.
    - That the factors and cardholder characteristics are monitored periodically to determine whether they effectively predict credit performance.
    - Whether the credit scores permit the bank to predict overall risk and the potential impact on collection activities.
    - Whether the models consider compliance with consumer laws and regulations. Refer any consumer compliance concerns to the OCC consumer compliance examiner.

2. Assess the reasonableness and adequacy of current underwriting standards and risk parameters used in scoring models.

3. Evaluate the adequacy of the scorecard revalidation.

4. Review override rates. If high, test a sample of low-end overrides to evaluate quality.

Marketing

1. Assess the level of risk associated with new product development. Consider:

    - The risks associated with different solicitation methods, such as preapproved versus take-one solicitations.
    - Feasibility studies.
    - Credit administration.
    - Compliance risk.

2. Review management's marketing and business plans to determine that the marketing program is structured to meet corporate strategic goals and objectives. Discuss any significant changes in account acquisition strategies with management.

3. Review the actual performance of the credit card operations compared with those presented in the marketing plan.

4.   Evaluate the reasonableness of market, economic, and profitability studies.

5.   Evaluate management's marketing program for secured cards, (or obtain from the examiner performing the marketing procedures), to determine:

- Whether the program has received appropriate approval.
- What media the bank uses to advertise its product.

New Accounts

Preapproved Account Solicitations and Underwriting

1.   Evaluate the bank's target market for the different products offered. Determine whether the bank's target market has changed. If so, evaluate how and why.

2.   Review the breakdown for the current year, and prior two years, of the bank's sources of new account acquisitions (percent of accounts that are preapproved versus those based on an application).

3.   Assess the level of risk assumed through preapproved account solicitations by obtaining copies of prior solicitation credit packages and evaluating the reasonableness of credit underwriting standards. Consider:

- The criteria management uses to select the names of solicited customers (both general exclusion and credit criteria).
- Whether credit criteria have changed significantly from previous mailings. If so, determine what management is hoping to achieve by any changes.
- Whether the bank uses credit bureau scores or proprietary scorecards. If so:
  - Determine the appropriateness of the cutoff scores used.
  - Determine what management hopes to achieve by the changes, if the cutoffs have changed since the last examination.
- Whether the distribution of names by credit criteria level and score ranges have changed from prior mailings. If they have changed, determine why and what the bank hopes to accomplish by the changes.
- The reasonableness of management's credit limits and whether any changes have occurred since the previous solicitations.

4.   Ensure that management extends a firm offer of credit to each consumer who accepts the preapproved offer of credit, with very limited exceptions.

5.   Evaluate the reasons provided by the bank for denying credit to a preapproved responder. (Refer to the Comptroller's compliance booklets for further guidance on presolicitations).

6.   Review delinquency and loss reports on a product-by-product basis to evaluate performance.

Application-based Account Acquisition and Underwriting

1.   Evaluate the bank's target market for the different products offered. Determine whether the bank's target market has changed. If so, identify how and why.

2.   Review the breakdown for the current year, and prior two years, of the bank's sources of new account

acquisitions (percent of accounts that are preapproved versus those based on an application).

3.   Determine whether the bank uses a judgmental process, automated scoring models, or a combination thereof to grant credit. (If the bank uses a scoring model, refer to the procedures in the "Scoring Models" section.)

4.   Make a judgement regarding the reasonableness of underwriting criteria.

5.   Review delinquency and loss reports on a product-by-product basis to evaluate performance.

Portfolio Acquisitions and Underwriting

1.   Evaluate the bank's target market for the different products offered. Determine whether the bank's target market has changed. If so, identify how and why.

2.   If the bank has recently purchased any credit card portfolios, review management's due diligence work papers to assess:

- The quantity of risk.
- The adequacy of the due diligence.
- Compliance with policy.

3.   Determine whether the bank conducts postmortems on acquired portfolios and, if so, review results.

4.   Review delinquency and loss reports on a product-by-product basis to evaluate performance.

Types of Credit Cards

Affinity and Cobranding Programs

1.   Determine whether any of the bank's affinity and cobranded programs:

- Diverge from the bank's normal underwriting standards.
- Offer preferential pricing.
- Offer features not available to other bank customers.

2.   If so:

- Evaluate the appropriateness of program differences, particularly relaxed underwriting guidelines.
- Determine the overall impact on portfolio quality and discuss your analysis with management.

3.   Review the terms of contracts with affinity groups or business partners to determine whether management has agreed to any inordinate or large concessions or contingent liability.

4.   If management had granted any inordinate or large concessions or assumed any contingent liability, investigate the reasons, particularly if the bank has only one or a few, large partners.

Corporate Card Programs

1.   Determine whether the bank has developed a strategic plan for the corporate program, and if so:

- Evaluate its adequacy.
- Determine whether the plan is consistent with management's overall strategic plan for credit card operations.

2.   Determine whether the bank offers cards to the company's employees for such items as travel expenses or to the company and its employees for procurement.

3.   If the corporation has liability for its corporate program with the bank, select a random sample of corporate card loan files. For each loan file:

- Review the borrower's financial condition. If management does not have a loan file, discuss the need to maintain adequate financial information.
- Determine compliance with the underwriting policy.
- Determine whether the bank risk rates the corporate card relationship and, if so, evaluate the accuracy of the assigned risk rating.

4.   Evaluate the level of past due corporate card accounts.

5.   Review a report listing accounts which are on a revolving payment plan to determine why these accounts are allowed to revolve.

6.   Review profitability reports and compare actual performance to budget. Discuss large or unusual variances with management.

Secured Credit Card Programs

1.   Determine whether the bank has developed a strategic plan for the secured credit card program and, if so:

- Evaluate its adequacy.
- Determine whether the plan is consistent with the bank's overall credit card strategic plans.

2.   Determine whether the bank's legal counsel has reviewed program forms to ensure the bank's perfection of a security interest in the deposit accounts.

3.   Select a random sample of secured credit card loan files. For each loan file:

- Determine compliance with the bank's underwriting policy.
- Check to see that credit lines are within the specified deposit amount, or that overlines received proper approval.
- Determine that a perfected security interest and proper controls exist over the deposit accounts.

4.   Determine whether the bank deals with independent sales organizations (ISOs). If so:

- Review the background checks performed on each ISO and its principals and salespeople.
- Review financial statements on each ISO to determine financial stability.
- Evaluate each ISO's level of involvement in the secured card program and determine whether the level of involvement is appropriate.
- Ensure that ISOs are not involved in underwriting decisions, approval of overlimits, collection activities, or

deposit control.
- Review the adequacy of contracts with ISOs.
- Review the appropriateness of compensation paid to ISOs and whether such compensation is tied to portfolio performance.
- Determine and evaluate the ISOs access to bank records, including the bank's data processing system.

5. If any ISO performs accounting services for the bank, determine its backup contingency plans and whether the bank could easily reconstruct data if the ISO fails, or the bank cannot otherwise access ISO systems.

6. Review a sample of marketing materials to determine:

- Whether the materials contain any information that could mislead consumers.
- Whether the bank's name is clearly evident on all marketing materials.

7. Evaluate the current level and trend of overline accounts in relation to the entire portfolio.

8. Review the past due report for secured credit cards. Determine the reasonableness of current past due volume.

Private Label Card Programs

1. Determine whether the bank has developed a strategic plan for the private label program. If so:

- Evaluate its adequacy.
- Evaluate whether the plan is consistent with the bank's overall credit card objectives.

2. Select a random sample of credit files including individual account files and retailer account files, to determine whether:

- Underwriting complies with the loan policy.
- The file has current financial information on the retailer.

3. Evaluate the level and trend of past due accounts in private label portfolios. Discuss with management any portfolios which exhibit deteriorating trends.

4. Review profitability reports on the private label department and compare actual performance to budget. Discuss significant variances with management.

5. If management recently purchased a private label portfolio, review work papers to assess the adequacy of their due diligence review and compliance with policy.

Account Management

1. Review reports detailing customer-initiated line increases and discuss trends with management.

2. If decisions are not automated, determine what credit criteria management uses for account management decisions, including line increases, renewals, and authorizations. Evaluate them for reasonableness.

3. If there is no clear process to ensure that line increases initiated by credit analysts (and requested by

customers) are made in compliance with internal guidelines, test a sample of manual line increases to determine that:

- They were processed according to guidelines.
- They are within approved lending authorities.

4. Request terms and account lists of cardholders with "no limit" lines of credit ("VIP" accounts) to determine whether reports and the performance of such accounts indicate that the program is sound.

5. Determine whether management uses screening techniques to review its cardholder base. If so:

- Evaluate what screens are used (behavior scoring, bankruptcy scoring, etc.).
- Identify for what purposes they are used.
- Identify what segments of the cardholder base are screened.
- Determine how often screening is done.

6. For each screening technique used:

- Evaluate program guidelines for reasonableness.
- If the entire base is not screened, determine how management selects the segments that are chosen.

Authorizations

1. If overlimit amounts are significant or if negative trends are evident, discuss with management.

2. Determine whether the level of overlimit accounts reflects effective control of transaction authorization and credit risk in general.

3. Make recommendations for improvement if appropriate.

Collections

1. Assess the effectiveness of the bank's overall collection strategies and the systems used to collect accounts. Consider:

- Whether such strategies are appropriate given the size and complexity of the operation.
- The bank's previous collection history.
- The bank's future marketing strategies.

2. Evaluate the various collection programs used, such as reaging, fixed payment, Consumer Credit Counseling Service (CCCS), and forgiveness. Specifically:

- Evaluate the collection programs in place and planned, through discussions with management.
- Evaluate the policies and procedures for each program and determine that management adequately monitors and analyzes the performance of each program.
- Assess the current and potential impact of such programs on the bank's reported performance and profitability, including ALLL implications.

3. Assess the adequacy of automated systems used by the bank to collect delinquent accounts. Discuss these

systems with management. Determine:

- Which automated collection system(s) the bank uses.
- How each system is used
- Key MIS reports generated by and for each system.

4. For each system, determine:

- That it provides sufficient data to allow collectors to make appropriate decisions.
- That the system generates a sufficient audit trail.
- That contingency plans are in place in the event of a temporary power outage or a disaster, and that the plans are tested on a regular basis.

5. If power-dialing is used to contact delinquent account holders, how the system routes "no contact" accounts.

6. Evaluate the bank's recoveries as a percentage of prior period losses by:

- Evaluating the accuracy of the figures.
- Determining whether recoveries fall within reasonable tolerances based on industry averages. If not, discuss with management and determine why recoveries were low.

7. Determine whether the bank is considered a debt collector as defined by the Fair Debt Collection Practices Act. If so, submit a memo to the EIC to ensure appropriate review at the next compliance examination.

8. Review the collection program for secured credit cards. Note any differences with the collection program as compared with other credit card programs.

9. Assess the appropriateness of management's incentive pay program for collectors. Pay particular attention to possible negative ramifications of such a plan (e.g., encourages protracted repayment plans, leads to aggressive reaging, or promotes individual rather than team efforts among the collectors.). Specifically:

- Evaluate how the program is administered.
- Determine whether the board or senior management reviewed and approved the incentive pay program in advance.
- Determine whether the plan limits the total incentive pay a collector may receive.
- Determine whether management compensates its collectors for placing accounts in various workout or fixed payment programs. If so, evaluate such activities for prudence.

Fraud

1. Review trends experienced in losses from fraud and evaluate whether losses compare with those being experienced by the industry. Discuss any atypical findings with management.

2. Review a delinquency aging report on accounts which have been blocked because of potential fraud concerns, as follows:

- Obtain all fraud block codes.
- Evaluate all accounts with such blocks.
- Classify accounts as appropriate.

Securitized Assets

1. Review reports detailing each outstanding securitized issuance and those in the pipeline, as follows:

    *   Determine significant terms of each securitized issue.
    *   Evaluate the current level and trends in the securitization process.
    *   Discuss with management their future expectations for additional securitized issuances.

2. Evaluate the performance of securitized issuances, and compare performance against early amortization triggers. Discuss significant trends in performance with management.

3. Evaluate the impact of collection programs, such as reaging, on performance reports to investors.

4. Review the terms of the securitization agreements to identify practices that may create liability or recourse on the bank's part. This might include preference to investors or credit enhancers in the receipt of payments.

5. If the bank routinely repurchases past due loans from the securitization, investigate the recourse implications (financing versus sales treatment).

6. Discuss with management the bank's plan to fund securitized assets upon maturity.

Purchased Credit Card Relationships

1. Determine whether the bank has booked any purchased credit card relationships (PCCR):

    *   If no PCCRs are booked, document in the working papers.
    *   If PCCRs are booked, complete questions 2 and 3 below, and questions 1 and 2 under "Quality - Processes; PCCRs."

2. Review all PCCRs and management's latest quarterly valuations and determine whether any are impaired. If any impairment exists, do not request a write-down without the specific authorization of the EIC.

3. Determine whether the bank uses a pool-by-pool approach or an aggregate approach to determine impairment.

The findings from the above questions regarding the adequacy of systems, controls, processes, and MIS, or if any PCCRs are impaired, will determine which of the following procedures, if any, should be completed to identify root causes of weaknesses/problems. Consult with the EIC to determine the need to expand the procedures based on the quantity of risk.

4. For portfolios with PCCRs, obtain and review the acquisition model(s) used in each purchase. Determine the type of model(s), such as discounted cash flow, capital flow, or a return on assets, management uses to acquire and value portfolios.

5. Determine how management uses the acquisition model(s).

6. Determine whether acquisition model(s) is/are well documented and periodically audited. If not, discuss with management and make recommendations.

7. For each model, determine whether the model was loaded with the final purchase contract terms.

    • If not, discuss with management the need for accurate final acquisition model(s) from which the true inherent discount rate can be determined.
    • If the premium used in the final acquisition model does not exactly match the premium used in the bank's PCCR amortization schedule, determine why.

8. If the model(s) is/are something other than a discounted cash flow model(s), evaluate the way management computed the inherent discount rate at the time of portfolio acquisition.

    • If no inherent discount rate was computed or an incorrect rate was used, determine the worthiness of the impairment test output.
    • Discuss with the EIC and management why the correct inherent discount rate must be maintained in order to conduct valuations correctly.

9. For each model, obtain and review the most recent valuation model used for the required quarterly impairment test. If the models are not discounted cash flow model(s) as required by call report instructions, discuss with EIC and management the possible need to recompute valuations using such a model.

    • Determine whether the discount factor used in each valuation model equals or exceeds the inherent discount factor used in the portfolio's acquisition.
       – If not, discuss the requirement of BB 93-16, "Intangible Assets – Final Capital Rule and Call Report Change," dated March 29, 1993, and call report instructions.
       – Discuss with the EIC and management the possible need to recompute the impairment tests using appropriate discount factors.

10. For each model, review the main drivers to ensure their reasonableness. Compare the drivers against prior period and/or prior year's actual statistics to determine reasonableness. If the drivers used in the quarterly valuation model(s) do not fairly represent recent trends, discuss with EIC and management to determine whether adjustments are required.

11. Review the amortization schedules for each model. Review the different types of intangibles in the PCCR, such as goodwill, yield adjustment, servicing rights, agreement not to compete, allowance for loan losses, broker's fees, agent bank relationship, etc. and perform the following:

    • Determine whether different amortization periods are used for each identified intangible (for example, 10 years for goodwill and 15 years for agent bank relationship). If any amortization periods exceed 10 years, discuss with the EIC and possibly the OCC accounting division to determine whether any adjustments are required.
    • Determine whether PCCRs are amortized using an accelerated amortization method.
       – If so, determine what the method is and how it corresponds to the value of the acquired asset, (e.g., 110 percent, 125 percent, 150 percent, 200 percent).
       – If a straight-line amortization method is being used, discuss with EIC and possibly the OCC accounting division to determine whether any adjustments are required.

12. Determine whether management has capitalized any ALLL expenses in conjunction with a portfolio acquisition (i.e., whether any of the intangibles are classified as allowance for loan losses). If so:

- Determine whether management has maintained the required documentation to allow for capitalization as required by the Bank Accounting Advisory Series (Purchase Accounting Adjustments, page 1C-2, June 1994).
- Discuss with the EIC and possibly the OCC accounting division to determine whether any adjustments are necessary, if the bank does not have documentation.

13. For each model, obtain and review the most recent quarterly fair market valuation (FMV) model to determine whether the PCCRs can be considered qualifying intangibles for regulatory capital purposes, as follows:

- Determine whether the discount factors used in the model(s) are appropriate market discount rates. If not, discuss with the EIC and management what possible range of rates would be more acceptable and the possible need to recompute FMVs.
- For capital purposes, determine whether the bank uses the lesser of (a) 90 percent of fair value, or (b) 100 percent of unamortized book value. If not, determine the significance and evaluate the possible need to amend call report(s).
- Determine that PCCRs included in regulatory capital do not exceed the permitted limit of 25 percent of Tier I capital.

Allowance for Loan and Lease Losses (ALLL)

1. Determine whether the allowance allocation for credit cards is an appropriate reflection of the inherent loss in the portfolio.

2. Review management's ALLL method for corporate card risk and ensure that it includes consideration of the financial condition of the underlying corporations, if applicable.

3. Determine whether the condition of private label credit card retailers is incorporated into the ALLL method.

4. Forward your findings/recommendations to the examiner assigned LPM/ALLL.

Reserving for Rebate Programs

1. Determine whether the issuer has any liability on any rebate program that it offers. If the issuer has no rebate liability, no further analysis is required. Document your findings in the working papers.

2. If the issuer is reserving for future redemption liability, review the general ledger account activity, and make a judgment about the adequacy of the reserve level based on redemption activity.

3. Determine, based on reviews of the financial condition of the issuers partners, whether any partner's financial condition may be questionable.

4. Review each product that has a rebate and for each program determine:

- The outstanding rebate reserve.
- The redemption volume in recent months.
- How the customer redeems the rebates.
- Whether outside vendors are used.

5.   Determine whether the contract limits the issuer's liability for certain items, such as rising airline ticket costs.

6.   In conjunction with the examiner performing the profitability analysis, determine the profitability of each product that is offering a rebate and compare against those that do not offer rebates.

Miscellaneous

1.   Review the bank's credit card strategic plan and determine whether management's plans for the department are clear and accurately reflect the current direction of the department.

Profit Analysis

1.   Review the most recent fiscal year-end and current year-to-date income statements.

2.   Review the most recent fiscal year-end and current year-to-date budgets and strategic plans. If actual financial performance varies significantly from budgeted or planned results, discuss reasons with management.

3.   Review the most recent strategic plan to determine what effects it will have on future profitability. If the plan indicates a material change from past practices, discuss with management.

4.   Review next year's budget. Determine whether the assumptions are reasonable and, if not, discuss with management.

5.   Analyze profitability on a managed asset basis. Make a summary judgement regarding profitability.

If your conclusions indicate poor financial performance, discuss with the EIC which of the following procedures need to be performed.

6.   Review income statements for each credit card program and portfolio and perform the following:

- Determine which programs are significant positive or negative contributors to profitability. Discuss with management as necessary.
- Review income and expense components to determine trends and their effect on current and future earnings.
- Determine whether any affinity or cobranding relationships exist and, if so, when contracts mature.
- Review affinity contracts for unusual financial requirements and/or payments.

7.   Determine what portion of the portfolio is fixed rate and what portion is variable rate.

- Discuss how often variable rate programs are repriced.
- Determine whether any repricing has been foregone or postponed.

8.   Determine what types and levels of fee-based income are received (i.e., annual membership fees, late fees, overlimit fees, bad check fees) and review fee income to determine trends.

9.   Discuss with management incoming interchange revenue and evaluate trends. Determine whether interchange is rebated and/or shared with any affinity or cobranding partners.

10. Determine whether the issuer retains any contingent liability from any rebate program. If so, determine its effect upon earnings, and determine whether management has established a rebate reserve associated with the program.

   - If they haven't, discuss with management.
   - If they have, review for appropriate reserve provisions and accuracy of reserve methodology.

11. Discuss with management other noninterest income levels and trends, such as from credit life insurance sales.

12. Discuss with management noninterest expense levels and trends. These could include:

   - Account acquisition and credit processing.
   - Card issuing.
   - Processing of incoming interchange.
   - Card holder billing.
   - Payment processing.
   - Card holder servicing and promotion.
   - Overlimit and collections
   - Issuer fraud investigation.
   - Card holder authorizations.
   - Issuer center administration.

13. Determine what, if any, corporate overhead is allocated to credit card operations and whether the level is appropriate.

14. Compare financial results against those reported by the industry and, if significantly different, determine causes.

Concentrations

1. Coordinate with the examiner responsible for "Concentrations of Credit" to ensure applicable procedures are performed.

Compliance with Laws, Rulings, and Regulations

1. Determine compliance with the following laws, regulations, and rulings pertaining to credit card lending:

   - Loans to Insiders – 12 USC 375a, 12 CFR and 12 USC 375b.
   - Records to be Retained by Financial Institutions – 31 CFR 103.33(a).

2. Determine whether the consumer compliance examination uncovered any violations where corrective action was necessary. Determine whether the violations were corrected.

Quality of Risk Management

Conclusion: The quality of risk management is (strong, satisfactory, weak).

Policy

Conclusion: The board (has/has not) established effective policies for credit card lending.

Objective: Determine the adequacy of the bank's credit card lending policies and procedures.

Scoring Models

1. Evaluate the adequacy of the bank's credit card scoring model policies. Policies should address the following:

    - Written guidelines. If policies are not written, consider whether they should be given the complexity of the bank's credit card operations.
    - Annual review and approval by the board.
    - The potential risks associated with credit card scoring models.

2. Determine whether the bank's override policy addresses both high- and low-end overrides and ensure that:

    - The policy clearly defines an override.
    - The policy requires that it be consistently applied.

Marketing

1. Evaluate the bank's credit card marketing policies. Policies should address the following:

    - Written guidelines. If policies are not written, consider whether they should be given the complexity of the bank's credit card operations.
    - Annual review and approval by the board.
    - The potential risks associated with credit card marketing.

New Accounts

Preapproved Account Solicitations and Underwriting

1. Determine whether management and the board have adopted written policies that:

    - Establish procedures for soliciting and reviewing credit card applications.
    - Define qualified borrowers.
    - Establish credit granting authority.

2. Review the board's written standards for setting credit limits for "up-to-offers" by determining whether:

    - The guidelines establish minimum and maximum lines of credit.
    - The guidelines require updated credit bureau reports before setting specific account limits.
    - Individuals with proper lending authority grant the credit limits.

- Supervisors approve exceptions.

Application-based Account Acquisitions and Underwriting

1.   Determine whether management and the board have adopted written policies that:

- Establish procedures for soliciting and reviewing credit card applications.
- Define qualified borrowers.
- Establish credit granting authority.

Portfolio Acquisitions and Underwriting

1.   Determine whether management and the board have adopted written policies that:

- Define qualified borrowers.
- Provide due diligence guidance.
- Address conducting "postmortems."

Types of Credit Cards

All Programs

1.   Review the bank's credit card policies. Determine whether the policies adequately address all functional areas including:

- Marketing.
- Underwriting.
- Portfolio administration.
- Collections.
- Charge-offs.

2.   For each individual credit card program policy, determine:

- If guidelines are written. If not, consider whether they need to be given complexity of the bank.
- That guidelines are reviewed and approved by the board.

Private Label Card Programs

1.   Review the bank's private label card policy. In addition to determining that the policy adequately covers topics listed in 1 and 2 above, ensure that the policy addresses:

- Portfolio purchases (including the due diligence process).

Account Management

1.   Review written policies and procedures governing account management activities. Determine whether policies are sufficient to cover significant account management activities and whether guidelines address, among other things, the following:

- Authority for approval of program and individual line increases, as well as permanent and temporary line increases.
- Credit criteria used to establish eligibility for line increases.
- Authority for overlimit authorizations, including permanent and temporary line increases, and credit criteria requirements.
- Standards for reinstatement and renewal of accounts.
- Coordination among marketing, legal, and credit personnel for account management activities.
- Standards for when credit bureau contacts are required.
- Standards for review and approval of customer-initiated line increases.
- Exception process for approvals outside of normal standards.

2. Determine whether management offers conditional line increases through the use of convenience checks. If so, determine whether credit criteria guidelines are reasonable.

3. Review criteria addressing decisions to reissue cards. Determine and discuss with management whether:

- Criteria are reasonable.
- Approval authority for renewal guidelines is appropriate.

4. Determine whether the bank offers "payment holiday" or "pay ahead" programs. If so:

- Obtain guidelines that identify how and to whom such programs will be offered.
- Identify credit criteria used to exclude eligible cardholders and evaluate for reasonableness.

5. Review eligibility criteria for cardholders with "no limit" lines of credit ("VIP" accounts) to determine whether the criteria are adequate to make a credit decision.

Collections

1. Assess the adequacy of the bank's written collection policies and procedures by ensuring that they sufficiently cover all necessary activities.

2. Evaluate the adequacy of the bank's charge-off policy by:

- Ensuring that it meets OCC and interagency policy guidelines.
- Reviewing the processor's user manual to verify that the charge-off parameters correspond to those described in the bank's charge-off policy. If not, discuss the differences with management and request appropriate corrective action.
- Determining how accounts scheduled for charge off are loaded into a charge-off queue or other system for loss. Specifically:
- Determine the circumstances, if any, which will delay an account charge-off.
- Determine whether the bank takes losses daily, weekly, or monthly.
- Ensuring that a payment of less than 90 percent of a full payment triggers advancement of the account to the next delinquency category. (This does not apply to fixed payment or workout program accounts for which the bank formally renegotiates terms.)

3. Assess appropriateness of fraud policies by determining:

- Whether possible fraud accounts are reaged before investigation.

- When fraud losses are realized.
- How fraud losses are taken (miscellaneous expense).

Securitized Assets

1. Evaluate the bank's asset securitization policy for adequacy.

2. Discuss with management the collection policies applied to the securitized portfolio.

3. If the bank routinely repurchases past due loans from the securitization, evaluate the recourse accounting policy to ensure it includes guidelines for following proper accounting (financing versus sales treatment).

Purchased Credit Card Relationships

1. Review the corporate/bank accounting manual and evaluate policies pertaining to PCCRs. Policy issues could include:

    - What type of models is to be used in the acquisition/valuation process.
    - Who approves the models.
    - How often valuations must be performed.
    - What range can be used for termination values used in the models.
    - What the maximum periods are that PCCRs may be amortized.
    - What amortization accounting method should be used.
    - How impairment will be determined (i.e., on a pool-by-pool or aggregate method basis).

2. If no policies exist, recommend development and adoption. If policies exist, but do not conform to regulatory parameters, recommend modification.

Miscellaneous

1. Review and evaluate the adequacy of any other miscellaneous credit card policies related to:

    - Risk Management.
    - Profitability.
    - Employee Accounts.

ALLL

1. Determine whether the board has approved an allowance for loan loss policy for the credit card operation and whether it is adequate in scope.

2. Review the issuer's internal accounting policies regarding rebate accounting and the rebate reserve method. If no policies exist, discuss with management the need for such policies and determine whether the issuer is reserving for rebate redemptions.

Processes

Conclusion: Management and the board (have/have not) established effective risk management processes for credit card lending.

Objective: To assess the quality of the bank's risk management systems related to credit card lending, including systems to identify, measure, monitor, and control risks.

Scoring Models

1. Evaluate the scoring system risk management process to ensure that:

   - It reflects current underwriting standards and risk parameters.
   - The scorecards are revalidated as necessary (review the report of the last revalidation).
   - It is supervised and maintained in accordance with vendor-provided specifications and recommendations (as specified in the scoring manual).
   - Management maintains a portfolio chronology log to record significant events related to the credit acquisition process (i.e., cutoff score changes, new marketing programs, new credit applications) for each portfolio.
     - If not, discuss the reasons with management and recommend they maintain a log.
     - If yes, review the log and discuss any significant changes with management.
   - Management is provided with the front and back-end MIS reports that are recommended by the vendor (such as population stability, characteristic analysis report, and delinquency distribution reports).

2. If generic scoring systems are used (such as those from credit bureaus), ensure that they:

   - Have been properly tested for the bank's population before implementation.
   - Are periodically monitored for effectiveness including, for example, revalidation or audit by an independent third party.

3. Determine whether the bank's override process addresses both high- and low-end overrides, and ensure that management:

   - Tacks the volume of both the high- and low-end overrides.
   - Monitors the effectiveness of the approved override policy (for example, tracks the performance of overridden accounts).
   - Calculates the override rate and ensures that it conforms to the vendor-specified method, if applicable.
   - Monitors the number of approved overrides.

Marketing

1. Evaluate management's system for reviewing marketing materials.

2. Evaluate how management controls marketing materials used by an Independent Sales Organization (ISO) if an ISO is the bank's marketing agent.

3. Evaluate management's process for developing and implementing marketing and business plans, by:

   - Noting time frames for activities and the approval process (who approved and when).
   - Determining how the plans address the stated direction and goals of the credit card operation and the bank as a whole.
   - Determining how the plans and the marketing process address credit, interest rate, and compliance risks.

- Assessing how they determine the appropriateness of the data used to develop the plans.
- Ascertaining whether management based their plans on any market, economic, or profitability studies performed either externally or internally.
- Determining whether plans incorporate scenarios under which credit standards will be liberalized or tightened.

4. Assess the new product development process and discuss with management. Specifically:

- Evaluate the review and approval process to ensure that all necessary participants are involved in product development before implementation, including:
    - Research and development (feasibility studies).
    - Credit administration.
    - Compliance management.
- Determine whether the planning process researches MIS needs and requires MIS to be adequate to supervise and administer products and verify that such systems are operative before product implementation.

5. Evaluate the internal controls employed to manage marketing and new product testing. Review the process to ensure that testing:

- Requires senior management's approval of a complete, supported testing plan that includes a determination that the proposed test meets, or is consistent with, the bank's strategic and business plan.
- Occurs using only very small populations, particularly in tests in which the bank is evaluating proposed changes in underwriting standards.
- Requires a thorough and well-supported "postmortem" analysis before implementing the change to a larger population.

New Accounts

Preapproved Account Solicitations and Underwriting

Objective: Assess the adequacy of front-end processes regarding preapproved account solicitations.

1. Discuss with management the prescreening solicitation process to:

- Determine the appropriateness of the bank's written procedures governing the prescreening process. If the bank does not have written procedures, discuss the need for such procedures with management.
- Determine whether management considers potential risks, including credit risk, transaction risk, interest rate risk, and compliance risks.
- Ensure that the risk management function has an appropriate role in developing the solicitation process, and effectively promoting sound underwriting principles.
- Determine who establishes the objectives for each mailing (such as the size of the mailing and response rates, amount of credit risk the bank is willing to assume, and overall profit objectives).
- Determine whether management has reviewed the results of previous solicitation programs before developing criteria and objectives for new solicitations.

2. Identify the bank's sources for preapproved account solicitations and how it chooses those sources (purchased list or credit bureau extract).

3.   From copies of prior solicitation credit packages, evaluate the reasonableness of the credit underwriting process as follows:

- Determine how management choose the credit criteria used to select the names of solicited customers.
- Determine the reasonableness of management's process for assigning credit limits.
- Determine whether management has procedures to prevent opening an excessive number of lines of credit for each customer.

4.   Determine whether management performs credit and marketing tests before full roll out. If so, determine whether management outlines the objectives of the tests in the solicitation program. (Note: The examiner reviewing the marketing function should also evaluate the testing process.)

5.   Determine whether management maintains a table showing its preference for certain credit bureaus based on the geographic locations targeted:

- If so, ensure that management periodically reviews and approves the table based on experience with the bureaus.
- If not, discuss with management the reasons for not using a table and recommend that it consider using them in the future.

6.   Evaluate the bank's process for ensuring that external vendors operate in accordance with bank instructions.

Objective: Assess the adequacy of back-end processes regarding preapproved account solicitations.

1.   Evaluate management's process to ensure that the bank extends a firm offer of credit to each consumer who accepts the preapproved offer of credit, with very limited exceptions.

2.   If risk management reviews the characteristics of the responders to determine whether the bank attracted the type of consumer it targeted, evaluate how.

3.   Determine whether management analyzes MIS reports (vintage reports) for preapproved accounts on a regular basis.

- If not, discuss the reasons with management and strongly recommend that it obtain and analyze vintage reports.
- If yes, evaluate the extent to which management uses this information to measure the success of the bank's programs and to refine strategies for future programs. Share comments regarding the reports with examiners performing examinations of the risk management and marketing functions.

Application-based Account Acquisitions and Underwriting

1.   Discuss with management the application process.

2.   Determine whether the bank uses a judgmental process, automated scoring models, or a combination thereof to grant credit. (If the bank uses a scoring model, refer to the procedures in the "Scoring Models" section.)

3.   Evaluate management's process for ensuring consistent application of the underwriting criteria.

Portfolio Acquisitions and Underwriting

1. Determine whether management has written procedures with respect to credit card portfolio acquisitions.

    - If so, determine whether the procedures are adequate in light of management's acquisition strategies and volume of acquisitions.
    - If the bank does not have procedures and periodically purchases credit card portfolios, discuss with the EIC and make an appropriate recommendation for development of written procedures.

2. Review management's due diligence process for acquiring a credit card portfolio. Determine how the bank consolidates and communicates findings of the due diligence review.

3. Assess management's process for conducting postmortems on acquired portfolios. Determine the intervals between postmortems and identify who receives the results.

Types of Credit Cards

Affinity and Cobranding Programs

1. Determine whether management has a formal process to evaluate prospective partners. The process should provide for assessing the financial condition and reputation of the endorsing association or company and for the profiling of prospective customers.

2. Evaluate the process by:

    - Reviewing documentation of a recent program to determine compliance with internal guidelines.
    - Discussing the need for such a process if none exists.

3. Determine whether the issuer uses a third party to identify and market to prospective partners. If so, determine:

    - Whether financial reviews of outside parties are periodically performed.
    - How the third party is compensated.
    - Whether the issuer performs audits of the marketing firm's operations.

Corporate Card Programs

1. Evaluate management's underwriting criteria/process for corporate credit cards by:

    - Considering:
        - The extent of financial information required from both the corporation and its individual employees, if applicable.
        - Underwriting guidelines.
        - Credit approval authorities.
        - Systems to ensure compliance with the underwriting process.
    - Ascertaining whether management or its corporate borrower decides which company employees receive corporate cards.
    - Determining how management sets credit limits on corporate cards.
    - Determining the system for approving overlimits.

- Determining the system for increasing and decreasing lines of credit.
- Determining whether management requires corporate guarantees.
- Determining the corporate card department's knowledge of whether the company also maintains a lending relationship with the commercial banking department.
- Determining whether communication between the corporate card and commercial banking departments is adequate.

2. Evaluate management's account monitoring system by determining:

- Responsibility for day-to-day account monitoring.
- The adequacy of MIS used in monitoring accounts.
- How often management reviews the financial condition of each corporation.
- Whether management has a tickler system for updating financial and other credit file data.
- Whether management monitors the profitability of each corporate card relationship.

3. Review management's system for approving revolving accounts.

Secured Credit Card Programs

1. Analyze management's process for underwriting secured credit cards by:

- Evaluating the credit application process from initial contact with the customer to issuance of the credit card and identifying parties and fees involved in the process.
- Evaluating management's requirements for approving an application.
- Determining how management sets credit limits.
- Determining how credit limits are increased and decreased.

2. Evaluate management's process for dealing with independent sales organizations (ISOs) by:

- Reviewing their system for ensuring that all salespeople are subject to a background investigation.
- Determining how they monitor the activities and performance of the ISO and whether such monitoring methods are adequate.
- Determining whether the ISO is involved with customer service and, if so, how management monitors the level and nature of customer complaints to the ISO.
- Determining management's system for ensuring compliance with Visa/MasterCard requirements concerning ISOs.

3. Review deposit account reports to determine:

- The adequacy of controls over deposits.
- If management routinely compares deposit accounts against outstanding credit lines.
- That deposit accounts are maintained separately and not co-mingled.

4. Obtain the overline account report and review the controls for approving overlines.

Private Label Card Programs

1. Evaluate management's underwriting process for private label credit cards, by determining:

- How management sets credit limits.
- Whether management reviews the financial condition of the retailer as part of its underwriting process.
- Whether management has any recourse arrangements with the retailer.
- Whether the private label department knows whether the retailer has a lending relationship with the bank's commercial banking department and, if so, whether communication between the departments is adequate.

2. Evaluate he system for increasing and decreasing credit lines.

3. Determine how management assigns risk ratings to private label relationships. If the retailer also has a commercial banking relationship with the bank, determine whether the risk ratings are consistent.

4. Evaluate the department's account monitoring system to determine:

- The scope and responsibility for account monitoring.
- How often the department analyzes the financial condition of retailers.
- Whether management has a system to ensure they regularly receive updated financial information on retailers.

5. Determine how management consolidates and communicates findings from due diligence reviews.

Account Management

1. Determine the process or processes management uses to ensure compliance with established guidelines. If processes do not exist or they are inadequate, make recommendations for improvement.

2. If management uses screening techniques to review their card holder base:

- Evaluate the process for assessing account management programs and strategies, such as use of adaptive control and "champion/challenger" systems. (See the section in Appendix A entitled "Adaptive Control.")
- Evaluate the process to review credit criteria and determine when management last reviewed and updated the criteria.

3. If the cardholder base is not screened regularly, discuss with management how they maintain a current credit risk profile for the card holder base.

4. Discuss the process to ensure that line increases initiated by credit analysts (and requested by customers) are made in compliance with internal guidelines. (This may include supervisor review of selected decisions or independent review.)

5. Determine whether an exception process exists to approve accounts that do not meet scoring or judgmental credit criteria (overrides). If so:

- Review reports that identify exceptions.
- Determine whether exceptions are reasonable and discuss any significant trends.
- Determine how the risk management function reviews exceptions.

6. Determine whether management offers conditional line increases using convenience checks. If so, determine

whether management has a process to test for adherence to credit guidelines.

7. Review the process for addressing decisions to reissue cards. Determine and discuss with management whether:

   - Guidelines are tested regularly.
   - Reissue/renewal strategies and controls are effective.

8. Evaluate management's procedures for reviewing credit lines when they become aware of a change in financial status or creditworthiness of a cardholder.

9. If management offers "payment holiday" or "pay ahead" programs, determine:

   - That an internal process exists to test such programs for compliance with internal guidelines.
   - How often the department reviews credit criteria and when management last revised its criteria.

10. For cardholders with "no limit" lines of credit ("VIP" accounts), determine:

    - Whether a process exists to identify minimum financial information requirements and to ensure that current financial information is obtained and analyzed.
    - Whether an internal process is in place to ensure that such accounts are offered on a limited basis to creditworthy customers.

Authorizations

1. Evaluate the overall adequacy of transaction authorization procedures and the effectiveness of such procedures for controlling credit risk.

2. Discuss with management how they ensure compliance with authorization guidelines.

3. Evaluate management's transaction authorization system by reviewing how:

   - Transaction limits are established with the bank card associations.
   - Transactions (if any) can be authorized by the intermediary network.
   - Transactions must come to the issuer for authorization.
   - Criteria are used to "block" accounts from transactions (i.e., communicated daily to the network).

4. Evaluate how transactions in excess of the credit limit are processed by:

   - Determining whether an established overline authorization limit has been established, and whether it is reasonable.
   - Determining what credit criteria are used to specify eligibility for overlimits, who approves the criteria, how often the criteria are reviewed and tested, and whether they are reasonable.
   - Identifying circumstances in which transaction requests are denied.
   - Determining the basis for any transaction approved by customer service for such approvals, and whether the approvals are reasonable.

Collections

1.   Assess the appropriateness of management's collection strategies by:

- Reviewing the method management uses to evaluate the effectiveness of its collection strategies.
- Determining who has authority to revise collection strategies after evaluating the conditions under which strategies may be changed.
- Evaluating how accounts are distributed to the collectors.
- Reviewing the number of accounts collectors handle on average, analyzing how this level is established, and determining whether it is appropriate.
- Establishing whether management uses behavior scoring or any other predictive techniques to assist in the collection of accounts. If so, determine:
  - Who built the system(s).
  - How the collection's department uses the system(s).
  - When the system(s) was/were last revalidated and by whom.
- Determining, if applicable, when the behavior scoring or other predictive systems trigger into a champion/challenger program (adaptive control). Specifically:
  - Determine who built the program(s).
  - Assess the adequacy of the policies and procedures governing the use of the program(s).
  - Ensure that the bank's controls provide for properly testing a challenger strategy before a decision is made to replace the current champion strategy.

2.   Evaluate the conditions under which management imposes a late fee on a delinquent account, the amount, and that they do not pyramid late fees.

3.   Determine the delinquency level at which management temporarily suspends further purchasing activity, and the level at which they close an account permanently. Specifically:

- Evaluate the circumstances under which a closed account can be reactivated, and verify that the collections department refers such accounts to the credit department for a decision.
- Determine whether behavioral scoring models generate or contribute to decisions to permanently cancel or temporarily suspend account activity. If so, assess the specific scoring ranges associated with each block.

4.   Review management's "skip tracing" practices and procedures to keep track of delinquent customers and determine their effectiveness by:

- Ascertaining what portion of the portfolio lacks current telephone numbers and mailing addresses.
- Determining whether management can monitor an outside agency used to skip trace accounts, if applicable.

5.   Determine what systems management uses to recover charged-off accounts and determine whether these systems interface with the bank's collection management system.

- If not, discuss how information is transferred from the collection management system to the recovery system.
- If the information is not transferred, assess how the recovery unit gathers and uses information about prior collection activities.

6.   Determine whether management uses outside collection agencies to recover accounts. If so:

- Evaluate the systems and controls used to supervise out placed accounts.
- Determine the frequency and how management rotates accounts between collection agencies.
- Determine how management monitors the success of collection agencies to ensure it is placing accounts with productive firms in the most cost-effective manner.

7. Determine whether management uses legal firms to recover accounts. If so:

- Determine what conditions trigger a referral to a legal firm.
- Determine how management decides which firms to use.
- Evaluate the systems and controls used to supervise accounts referred to legal firms.
- Evaluate the costs associated with the use of legal firms.

Fraud Control

1. Evaluate systems and controls used in the fraud control function. Make a summary judgement regarding fraud control.

Note: If your conclusions indicate poor management of the fraud function, discuss with the EIC which of the following procedures, if any, need to be completed.

2. Evaluate how management reports and handles initial conversations with account holders regarding potential fraudulent activities. Specifically:

- Determine whether customer service or collections handle fraudulent activities.
- Determine whether potential fraudulent issues are transferred immediately to fraud control.
- Review the flow chart or outline the process for handling potential fraud cases.
- Determine whether a bank employee could have been involved.
- Determine whether a review of the bank's controls of issued cards is completed.
- Determine that signatures on sales drafts are compared to signatures on notifications for owners of cards disclaiming knowledge of sale or loss of card.
- Determine that an officer is required to sign off on the conclusion of the fraud investigation.

3. Discuss with management special processes to reduce the potential for fraud. These could include:

- Outside mail sorting.
- Issuing credit cards for longer periods.
- Reviewing all payment checks over a given amount.
- Increasing fraud training.
- Ensuring management is knowledgeable about bank card associations' fraud programs.

4. Evaluate the process for determining whether, and when, skip tracing is triggered after a suspect has been identified, but the bank has been unable to contact the suspect.

5. Evaluate if and how charged off fraud accounts are handled in recovery.

6. Determine whether internal audit is notified of all potential frauds in accounts.

Securitized Assets

1. Discuss with management how they determine accounting treatment for securitized assets.

2. Discuss with management their planning process to ensure there are adequate systems for servicing current and anticipated securitizations.

Purchased Credit Card Relationships

1. Evaluate management's modeling and accounting processes by discussing them with bank personnel.

2. If systems, controls, processes, or MIS are inadequate, or PCCRs are impaired, consult with the EIC to determine the need to expand "Quantity" procedures to identify root causes of weaknesses/problems.

3. Evaluate how senior management reviews and approves credit card portfolio acquisition model(s). If they are not reviewed, recommend formal review and approval.

Miscellaneous

1. Determine where and how the risk management function is performed for the credit card operation.

2. Assess the adequacy of the function. In conjunction with examiners reviewing the various functional areas, determine whether risk management takes an appropriate role in:

   - Developing and maintaining underwriting and account management guidelines, including monitoring adherence thereto.
   - Developing and implementing marketing initiatives and the new product development process.
   - Ensuring the integrity of the scoring systems and other models in use.
   - Reviewing significant policies and procedures, including revisions, for adequacy and to assess their impact on portfolio quality.
   - Ascertaining the quality of the portfolio and assigning appropriate risk grades.
   - Identifying potential risks, including compliance risks, arising from concentrations of credit (corporate card, affinity, and cobranding programs) and lending limits.
   - Performing and reviewing analyses to be able to assess various marketing, credit scoring models, and account management strategies.
   - Recommending appropriate changes to collections including changes to management, staffing, or practices.

Profit Analysis

1. Determine management's process for analyzing credit card portfolio profitability. The process should include:

   - The preparation of a budget by:
     - Function.
     - Program.
     - Overall Operation.
   - Actual results compared to budget at least monthly.
   - The identification of significant trends and deviations, which are adequately explained in the financial review process.

2.	Determine whether management has systems in place to evaluate profitability at the account level. If no system is in place, review with management how they determine when to waive annual fees and when to charge or refund punitive fees. Also, determine how management allocates monies and time to account retention programs.

3.	Evaluate how receivables are funded and determine if profits are susceptible to volatility due to funding strategies (i.e., using daily funds), as follows:

- Discuss the issue with an OCC capital markets expert, for complex operations.
- Determine interest rate risk being taken by the issuer.

4.	Discuss with management how pricing is established for each program.

5.	Review finance charge income to determine trends and whether management uses introductory rates, teaser rates, or rate sales to market products. If so:

- Discuss with management the impact these pricing strategies will have on future net interest margins.
- Ensure that management has appropriate MIS in place to estimate the impact of these marketing decisions on profitability.

Employee Accounts

1.	Determine the reasonableness of management's procedures for establishing employee accounts.

2.	Evaluate management's process for reviewing employee accounts.

ALLL

1.	Review the bank's credit card allowance method and assess its reasonableness by using the most recent quarter-end report.

2.	Evaluate whether management's analysis is documented and properly recognizes the risks in the portfolio.

3.	Evaluate the process management uses to incorporate secured credit card overline accounts in its ALLL methodology.

Reserving for Rebate Programs

1.	Evaluate how the issuer reviews the financial condition of its partners.

2.	Evaluate the rebate reserve method for each program and decide whether the method is reasonable. Determine whether:

- Actual performance is reasonable compared with pro forma financial data.
- Management adjusts the rebate reserve assumptions based on actual experience.

3.	Determine whether the issuer uses outside vendors to manage the redemption process. If so, determine:

- Whether the financial condition of the vendor is known and periodically reviewed.
- How the vendor is paid.
- The frequency of information exchanges.
- Whether the issuer performs periodic audits of the vendor's operation.
- Whether cardholders know they are dealing with a vendor.

4.   Evaluate the maturity date of contracts and determine how the issuer will manage such items as overhead if the contract is terminated at maturity. Determine whether any extension periods are permitted.

Personnel

Conclusion: The board, management and effected personnel (do/do not) possess the skills and knowledge required to manage and perform duties related to credit card lending.

Objective: Given the size and complexity of the bank, determine if bank management/personnel possesses and displays acceptable knowledge and technical skills in managing and performing credit card lending functions.

1.   For each credit card lending functional area, assess the structure, depth, and experience of management, key personnel, and staffing by:

- Reviewing the organizational chart in conjunction with management's resumes.
- Reviewing any management-prepared staffing analyses and determining if staffing levels are adequate considering present and future plans.
- Ascertaining management's knowledge of current policies and procedures through discussions and the results of the completion of these procedures.
- Evaluating previous credit card related lending, administrative, and collection experience.

2.   Specifically evaluate the experience of management and the staff in Corporate Card Lending and Private Label Lending by:

- Reviewing management's resumes to determine whether their experience is balanced between marketing and credit.
- Determining whether the staff has commercial lending analysis experience (for reviewing the financial stability of the retailer).
- Determining whether a credit analysis is prepared and reviewed by the commercial department, if the private label department does not have commercial lending expertise.

3.   Assess the adequacy of the structure, management, and staffing in the Collections area. Consider:

- Collector and supervisor experience levels.
- Staff openings
- Ratio of accounts to collectors.
- Ratio of collectors to supervisors.
- Delinquency levels and trends.
- Portfolio growth.
- The quality and depth of the staff in the fraud control department, based on the size and complexity of the issuer.

4. Assess the adequacy and effectiveness of management's training program for collectors by:

    - Reviewing a copy of the training manual, on-the-job training programs, and supervisory follow-up and monitoring.
    - Discussing alternative means of training with management. If the bank's circumstances warrant a more formal training process, make appropriate recommendations.

5. Determine if bank officers and employees are operating in conformance with policies and processes.

6. Assess management's ability to manage credit card lending based on the results of the quantity of risk and quality of risk procedures.

Controls

Conclusion: Management (has/has not) established effective control systems relating to credit card lending.

Objective: Determine the scope and adequacy of control systems used to monitor credit card lending.

Scoring Models

1. Determine whether management periodically audits the application scoring models to ensure that:

    - Data from the applications are being inputted properly.
    - The application system is scoring the information correctly.
    - The scope and frequency of the audits are reasonable.
    - Credit lines are periodically reviewed.

Marketing

1. In discussion with executive management, identify the control mechanisms used to monitor marketing plans and activities.

2. Assess new product development control systems and discuss with management.

    - Determine that appropriate feasibility studies are performed before the products are implemented.
    - Determine that credit administration has an appropriate role in the development process.
    - Assess controls in place to ensure that compliance issues are considered when all new products are being developed.

3. Review copies of the marketing reports provided to and used by senior management to assess the performance of marketing initiatives.

    - Evaluate for adequacy and accuracy.
    - Determine that the reports contain sufficient detail within which to evaluate the performance and profitability of each individual marketing initiative.

4. Review copies of the reports generated by and used within the department to control and monitor marketing initiatives. Assess for adequacy and accuracy.

5.   Assess the adequacy of the audit function employed in the marketing area, using the most recent audit, regulatory, and other reports which may impact the marketing area.

- Determine the adequacy of the scope, timing, and frequency of the audits or internal reviews performed.
- Assess the adequacy and timeliness of corrective action taken by management in response to significant findings.

6.   Evaluate department procedures for performing audits or otherwise reviewing the controls and procedures of outside vendors, including credit bureaus. Assess for adequacy by:

- Reviewing a sample of recent vendor audits to determine adherence to the bank's procedures.
- Reviewing the scope, timing, and frequency of the vendor audits.
- Determining the adequacy of the bank's follow-up procedures for ensuring prompt and effective corrective action in response to deficiencies disclosed during the audit process.

New Accounts

Preapproved Account Solicitations and Underwriting

1.   Review the latest loan review done by the loan review department for adequacy. Determine if appropriate corrective actions have been made on deficiencies noted. Consider:

- Front-end process regarding preapproved account solicitations.
- Back-end process regarding preapproved account solicitations.

2.   Assess the scope and adequacy of the latest internal/external audit. Determine if appropriate corrective actions have been made on deficiencies noted.

- Determine whether management completes audits to ensure that:
  - The names originated by the credit bureau meet original exclusion and credit criteria (both accepted and rejected names).
  - Mail vendors print preapproved coupons in accordance with instructions (name and addresses, credit limits, expiration date, etc.).
- Verify that the bank performs an audit to ensure that data from the response coupon is input correctly into the account processing system. Determine the scope and frequency of the audit.

3.   Determine the adequacy of any other control systems employed to manage preapproved account solicitations.

Application-based Account Acquisitions and Underwriting

1.   Assess the scope and adequacy of the latest internal/external audit and loan review. In addition to the adequacy of scope, coverage, frequency, etc. of these functions, determine that:

- Underwriting standards are checked for compliance.
- Credit limits are checked for appropriateness.

2.   Determine that appropriate and timely corrective actions have been taken on identified deficiencies.

3. Verify that the bank performs an audit to ensure that data from the application is inputted correctly into the account processing system.

4. Evaluate the adequacy of any other control systems employed to manage application-based account acquisitions.

Portfolio Acquisitions and Underwriting

1. Assess the scope and adequacy of the latest internal/external audit and loan review. Determine if appropriate corrective actions have been made on deficiencies noted.

2. Determine the adequacy of any other control systems employed to manage portfolio acquisition activities.

Types of Credit Cards

Affinity and Cobranding Programs

1. Assess the adequacy of control systems employed to manage the affinity and cobranding programs in the following areas:

   - Loan review.
   - Audit.
   - Compliance review.
   - Any other control systems used by management.

2. Review internal reports which are used to monitor affinity or cobranded programs. Programs should be tracked individually. If not, discuss with management the need for such reports.

3. Determine whether internal reports are adequate and consider issues such as:

   - Program profitability.
   - Average utilization rates.
   - Average response and approval rates.
   - Average credit limits.
   - Program delinquencies and charge-offs.
   - Average behavior or bureau scores.

Corporate Card Programs

1. Assess the adequacy of control systems employed to manage the corporate card programs in the following areas:

   - Audit.
   - Compliance review.
   - Any other control systems used by management.

2. Determine whether loan review performs a periodic review of credit quality and loan administration for corporate cards.

---

3.   If the corporate borrower decides which employees receive cards, evaluate what controls the bank uses to reduce risk.

Secured Credit Card Programs

1.   Assess the adequacy of control systems employed to manage the secured credit card programs in the following areas:

- Loan review.
- Audit.
- Compliance review.
- Any other control systems used by management.

2.   Assess the bank's control systems employed to manage independent sales organizations (ISOs) activities.

- Review the bank's last review of internal controls at the ISO. Inquire as to the frequency of the bank's onsite inspection of ISOs.

3.   Review MIS reports for the secured card program to determine:

- Whether such MIS reports are sufficient to keep management adequately informed about the condition of the program.
- Whether the bank tracks secured card performance separately from its other credit card programs.
- How MIS reports are generated and verified for accuracy.

Private Label Card Programs

1.   Assess the adequacy of control systems employed to manage the private label card programs in the following areas:

- Audit.
- Compliance review.
- Any other control systems used by management.

2.   Determine whether loan review performs a periodic review of the private label portfolio, including the credit quality of the retailer and loan administration.

Account Management

1.   Assess the adequacy of control systems employed to manage account management activities in the following areas:

- Loan review.
- Audit.
- Compliance review.

2.   Review management reports used to evaluate the effectiveness of account management practices and programs.

- They may include information regarding utilization rates, purchase volume, fee income, delinquencies, charge-offs, etc.
- Exception reports that include credit card extensions, renewals, or other factors that would result in a change in customer account status.

3.   If the bank offers "payment holiday" or "pay ahead" programs, review analyses or reports which measure the impact of such programs. Determine whether they are adequate and discuss your analysis with management.

Authorizations

1.   Review internal reports on overlimit activity to verify that they include the percentage of accounts in an overlimit status as well as the percentage of dollars in the portfolio in an overlimit status.

Collections

1.   Assess the adequacy of audit and loan review in the collections area (i.e., scope, frequency, timing, report content, and independence), and management's response to previous deficiencies identified by:

- Reviewing the most recent audits (internal and external) as well as pertinent reports submitted by loan review and/or bank consultants.
- Evaluating the adequacy and timeliness of management's response to any significant issues dealing with accounting, policies and procedures, or collections programs disclosed in these reports. If necessary, test corrective action.
- Discussing any necessary audit enhancements with management and the loan portfolio management (LPM) examiner.

2.   Assess the quality, accuracy, and completeness of MIS reports and other analyses used to manage the collections process. Specifically:

- Evaluate the quality of MIS collection reports provided to executive management on a regular basis.
- Determine whether the reports provide adequate data upon which to base informed decisions.
- Determine the appropriateness and accuracy of key collection reports.

3.   Review MIS reports pertaining to fraud control. Determine:

- The usefulness of the information presented.
- The level of fraud losses as compared with industry averages.

Securitized Assets

1.   Assess the adequacy of the control systems employed to manage securitization of assets in the following areas:

- Loan review.
- Audit.
- Any other control systems used by management.

2.   Evaluate the adequacy of MIS for the securitization process at both the board and management level.

Purchased Credit Card Relationships

1.   Assess the adequacy of the control systems employed to manage PCCR in the following areas:

- Loan review.
- Audit.
- Any other control systems used by management.

Miscellaneous

1.   Review internal MIS reports and determine whether they adequately inform management of the condition of the department.

2.   Review the monthly financial information (profitability analysis) provided to senior management. Evaluate its usefulness and accuracy.

Conclusion

Objective: Determine overall conclusions and communicate examination findings regarding the quality of risk and risk management systems in credit card operations.

Objective: Initiate corrective action when policies, practices, procedures, or internal controls are deficient or when violations of law, rulings, or regulations have been noted.

1. Provide the LPM examiner or EIC a brief conclusion memo regarding the quality, level, and direction of risk, and the adequacy of risk management systems. Consider findings in the following areas:

   - Scoring Models
   - Marketing
   - New Accounts
   - Types of Cards
   - Account Management
   - Collections
   - Allowance for Loan and Lease Losses
   - Securitized Assets
   - Purchased Credit Card Relationships
   - Miscellaneous Credit Card Procedures

2. If applicable (i.e., for credit card banks), determine the [CAMELS] Component Rating. Consider:

   - Adequacy of underwriting standards, soundness of credit administration practices, and appropriateness of risk identification practices.
   - The level, distribution, severity, and trend of problem, classified, restructured, delinquent, and nonperforming assets.
   - The adequacy of the allowance for loan and lease losses.
   - Credit risk arising from off-balance sheet transactions.
   - The diversification and quality of the credit card portfolio.
   - Concentrations.
   - The adequacy of credit card policies, procedures, and practices.
   - The ability of management to properly administer assets.
   - The adequacy of internal controls and management information systems.

3. For banks with a composite CAMELS rating of 1 or 2, provide the EIC with brief conclusions regarding the following topics. For banks with a composite CAMELS rating of 3 or worse (i.e., there is increasing or high levels of problem assets and risk which require an elevated level of supervisory concern), conclusions should be more detailed. They should address the less than satisfactory asset quality or credit administration practices that exist along with detailed conclusions on the following areas:

   - The quantity of risk.
   - The quality of the bank's risk management systems, including systems to identify, measure, control, and monitor risks.
   - The quality of operations (including the adequacy of policies, practices, procedures, and internal controls) and the adequacy of management information systems.
   - Whether programs are structured to meet corporate strategic goals and objectives, the department is

operating profitably, and bank officers are operating in conformance with the established guidelines.
- Compliance with applicable laws, rulings, and regulations.
- Recommended corrective action when policies, practices, or procedures are deficient.
- Commitments received from bank management to address concerns.

4. For banks with a composite CAMELS rating of 3 or worse ONLY; provide a detailed conclusion comment to the EIC discussing:

- The root causes of problems.
- Factors that contributed to the less than satisfactory condition.
- Management's ability to correct the bank's fundamental problems.
- Strategies to address the bank's weaknesses (in consultation with the EIC).

5. Determine the impact on the aggregate and direction of risk assessments for any applicable risks identified by performing the above procedures. Examiners should refer to guidance provided under the OCC's large and community bank risk assessment programs.

- Risk Categories: Compliance, Credit, Foreign Currency
    Translation, Interest Rate, Liquidity, Price,   Reputation, Strategic,
    Transaction
- Risk Conclusions: High, Moderate, or Low
- Risk Direction: Increasing, Stable, or Decreasing

6. Determine in consultation with EIC, if the risks identified are significant enough to merit bringing them to the board's attention in the report of examination. If so, prepare items for inclusion under the heading Matters Requiring Board Attention. Refer to the Comptroller's Bank Supervision Process booklet for determining the appropriateness of MRBA's.

7. Discuss findings with management including conclusions regarding applicable risks. Consider:

- The quality of risk management systems in terms of identifying controlling, monitoring, and managing risks.
- The quality of departmental management.
- The adequacy of policies relating to credit card lending.
- The manner in which bank officers conform to established policy.
- Adverse trends within credit card lending.
- Internal control deficiencies or exceptions.
- The accuracy and completeness of the schedules obtained from "loan portfolio management."
- Delinquent loans, including a breakout of "bad debts" as defined by 12 USC 56.
- Violations of laws, rulings, and regulations.
- Extensions of credit to major shareholders, employees, officers, directors, and/or their interests.
- Other matters regarding the condition of the department.
- Recommended corrective action when policies, practices, or procedures are deficient.
- Other matters of significance.

8. As appropriate, prepare a brief credit card/asset quality comment for inclusion in the report of examination. Consider:

- The quantity of risk.

- The quality of risk management.

9. Prepare a memorandum or update the work program with any information that will facilitate future examinations.

10. Update all applicable OCC electronic information systems and any applicable report of examination schedules or tables.

11. Organize and reference working papers in accordance with OCC guidance.

Credit Scoring

Development of Scoring Models

Multiple linear regression analysis is the statistical technique most commonly used to develop a credit scoring model. In this approach, coded characteristics from loan applications or credit bureau reports and other relevant documents are inputted into a computer program to predict the likelihood with 95 percent confidence that a credit card account will perform as agreed. The model uses those factors correlating most strongly with good or bad performance. Data from applications previously rejected for credit are also analyzed statistically to predict what their performance would have been had they been accepted.

Scoring models are only as good as the sample from which they are drawn. They predict the behavior of new applicants based on the performance of previous applicants. Models are also limited because inferences about the performance of previously rejected applicants are included in the sample. Other elements affecting a model's ability to rank order risk arise from using different sources to select sample applicants, using new market area data, and/or changing credit policy. Also, economic or regulatory changes can impact the reliability of the model.

Models are rescored prior to system implementation to validate the ability to rank order risk as designed. The validation process ensures the demographic profiles of current applicants, or names selected for prescreening, are similar to those used in the sample. It also measures the divergence between two populations; i.e., through-the-door applications versus the development sample used to build the model, and sets credit scoring norms to account for slight shifts in the population credit score. The Chi-Square, Kolomogorov-Smirnov, and the Stability Index are the most common statistical validation tests used by banks.

Rescoring credit scores prior to implementation is important. It helps detect potential problems early on rather than waiting for 12 to 18 months after accounts are booked. Waiting to determine the actual performance of new accounts could seriously threaten the creditworthiness of the portfolio.

Scoring models generally become less predictive as time passes. Certain characteristics about an applicant, such as income, job stability, and age change over time as do overall demographics. One-by-one, these changes will result in significant shifts in the profile of the through-the-door population. Once a fundamental change in the profile occurs, the model is less able to identify potentially good and bad applicants. As these changes continue, the model loses its ability to rank order risk. Thus, a credit scoring model is redeveloped as necessary.

After the scoring system is implemented, its developer provides bank management with a manual that details system maintenance requirements and recommended methods for supervising the system. Bank management should adhere closely to manual specifications, particularly those that provide guidance for periodically assessing performance of the system. This often includes comparing actual results to system objectives.

For systems developed by outside vendors, examiners should review vendor guidelines in conjunction with bank management's system for periodically assessing the system and the frequency of such assessments. One quick way to evaluate the general performance of a system is to determine whether a direct correlation exists between credit scores and delinquency rates (that is, delinquency rates increase as risk increases). Another way is to review the management reports described later in this appendix.

Types of Scoring Systems

Application Scoring

Systems that rely on data from credit applications are the most commonly used types of systems in credit scoring. Key items of application information (and credit bureau information, when available) are assigned point values. Typical application data include: continued employment over a period of time, length of time in a credit bureau file, and rent or mortgage payments over a period of time. The characteristics selected to predict the ability to repay a credit card loan assigned point values are income, debt-to-income ratios, occupation, and outstanding credit balances. Banking references, credit references, reported delinquencies, recent credit bureau inquiries, and recently opened accounts are assigned point values which reflect a consumer's use of credit. Terms such as amount of loan, percent down, and purpose of the loan are also factored into the scoring. The total of these point values (final score) reflects the relative likelihood that the consumer will repay as contracted.

Credit Bureau Risk Scoring

The goal of using a credit bureau risk scoring system is to achieve superior predictive power. An individual's application is sent to one of the bureaus for scoring based on the contents of the application and previous payment history in his or her credit bureau report. The system statistically ranks current elements of a credit report to predict the customer's future credit payment behavior. Because of the depth of information available, credit bureau data elements tend to have better success rank ordering risk or bankruptcy than other systems.

Banks purchase these scores for use in applicant screening, account acquisition, and account management strategies:

• Applicant screening B for approving or declining the loan, establishing initial credit limits, and setting up a tiered pricing of loans.

• Account acquisition B used in solicitation programs, cross-selling opportunities of other products, and for acquiring portfolios from other institutions.

• Account management B for determining increases and decreases of credit limits, and establishing authorizations, reissue, and collections parameters.

Bureau scores are designed to predict overall losses by classifying accounts into "good" and "bad" groups. A "good" account is one with no delinquencies or an isolated delinquency. A "bad" account includes serious data relating to delinquency, bankruptcy, charge-off, or repossession.

Each bureau's scorecards are revalidated every 18 to 24 months. Over 100 predictive variables are evaluated during the development or redevelopment cycle. Such variables include: previous credit performance, current level of indebtedness, amount of time credit has been in use, pursuit of new credit, and types of credit available.

Scorecard vendors have risk scorecards in place at the major credit bureaus. The vendor uses the same process at each bureau to update and validate the scorecards. Generally, vendors evaluate the individual's performance at the time of revalidation and 24 months ago. The earlier of these reports is used to generate the predictive information, and the later one, dated 24 months later than the first, is used to determine the performance of that account in the two years since the observation of the predictive information.

Credit Bureau Bankruptcy Scoring

Bankruptcy scorecards are primarily used to predict the likelihood that a customer will declare bankruptcy or become a collection problem at some point. Credit bureaus apply bankruptcy scorecards to information in a consumer's credit file containing credit histories from all reporting sources.

Several bankruptcy scorecards are usually available at each credit bureau.

Credit Bureau Revenue Scoring

Revenue scores are designed to rank order prospects by the amount of net revenue likely to be generated on a new bankcard account in the first 12 months. Revenue scores are available through the credit bureaus. The models are built using master file information on the amount of revenue generated on a bankcard account in the 12-month performance period using high balance to limit ratios, significant revolving balances, and multiple bankcards in use.

Behavioral or Performance Scoring

Behavioral scoring is a technique used to segment a portfolio of existing accounts based on the past behavior of the borrowers. Banks use behavioral scores for collection strategies, authorization requirements, credit line assignments, and renewal decisions. This scorecard predicts which accounts will become delinquent within the next six to 12 months. Behavioral scoring relies principally on credit line usage patterns (revolving credit) and payment patterns. Behavioral scoring models consider elements like payment history, the number of times the payment has been greater than the minimum required, delinquency history, and use of the cash advance option. Credit bureau input may also be used.

Emerging neural net technology has enhanced the effectiveness of behavioral modeling. Neural nets are computer programs that can sort through mammoth amounts of data and spot patterns, mimicking human logic patterns. Neural nets predict better than current behavioral scoring models the accounts that can handle an increase in credit limits and those that cannot. The principal advantage of a neural net is that, like humans, it learns from previous experience. This knowledge is then factored into subsequent decisions.

Collections Scoring

Other scoring models are devoted mainly to collection activities. They include:

Collection scoring B These systems show the likelihood that collection efforts will succeed. They help a bank allocate collection resources efficiently.

Payment projection scoring B These systems identify the likelihood that a bank will receive a payment on a delinquent account within six months. The collections area can use this information to determine which accounts should be "worked."

Recovery scoring B These systems identify the likelihood of recoveries after charge off. The collections area can use these systems to minimize charge-off losses.

Adaptive Control

Banks can use behavioral scoring to examine alternative credit strategies. These strategies employ a technique called "adaptive control." Adaptive control systems include software that allows management to develop and analyze various strategies which take into account the customer population and the economic environment. Adaptive control systems are credit portfolio management systems designed to reduce credit losses and increase promotional opportunities. New strategies (called challenger strategies) can be tested on a portion of the accounts while retaining the existing strategy (called the champion strategy). When a challenger strategy proves more effective than the existing champion, the bank will replace the champion strategy with the challenger. Continual testing of alternative strategies can help the bank achieve better profits and control losses in five possible areas:

- Credit line management B Current and delinquent accounts are reviewed for credit line and cash line increases and decreases at billing, based on several timing options.

- Delinquent collections B All accounts are checked for delinquency at billing time. Delinquent accounts are evaluated and actions are assigned to be taken throughout the next month. For example, computer-generated notices can be sent to account holders at varying intervals for 30 days; if the account remains delinquent, collectors can make phone calls every five days. Delinquent accounts are then reexamined for a change in account status. If there is no change, assigned actions proceed. If an account is no longer delinquent, actions are stopped. Accounts also can be reevaluated and assigned different actions (called dynamic reclassification).

- Overlimit collections B Accounts are examined for overlimit action at billing and posting. At billing, an overlimit account may be sent a notice. Additional action may be taken based on the overlimit scenario.

- Authorizations B Accounts are examined at billing and assigned an authorization strategy to be used by the authorization system throughout the month. The authorization system requests a decision on accounts in early delinquency or overlimit status.

- Reissue B Accounts are reviewed for reissuance at a certain time. This can be done a number of times a year and some action, such as mailing letters as to the status of cards or sending a new credit card, can be taken.

Strategies for Selecting and Changing Cutoff Score

Three strategies may be used either separately or together to select the cutoff score. The first strategy targets an approval or acquisition rate. The cutoff is set to result in a specified number of new accounts. Used separately, this may be the least desirable approach since it does not capture any projected performance of the accounts. The second strategy targets a credit loss rate. A cutoff score is selected which sets an acceptable level of losses. The third strategy targets the product's profitability. A cutoff score can optimize expected profitability in terms of total profit center earnings, return on risk assets, or return on total assets.

The following are some of the most common reasons for changing a credit cutoff score:

- To approve previously declined accounts that are now believed to be potentially profitable.

- To decline previously approved accounts that are now observed to be unprofitable.

- To reduce losses and/or improve collections.

- To respond to increased or reduced competition in the marketplace.

- To comply with external suasion to ease or restrict credit availability.

- To compensate for aging and/or eroding scoring models.

Management Reports

Population stability report B This report measures changes in applicant score distribution over time. The report compares the current application population and the population on which the scoring system was developed by using a formula called the "population stability index." The index measures the separation of the two distributions of scores. (The scoring manual has instructions on how to interpret the variances.) For example, in a commonly used scorecard, a value under 0.100 indicates that the current population is similar to the original and no action is necessary. A value between 0.100 and 0.250 suggests management should research the cause of the variance. A value over 0.250 suggests that substantial change has occurred in the population or the policies.

Characteristic analysis report B This report measures changes in applicants' scores on individual characteristics over time. It is needed when the population stability has changed and the bank wants to determine which characteristics are being effected. The report compares individual characteristics of the current applicants with those of the original development population. For example, checking and savings account references may be a better predictor of future behavior when the applicant has more history with the same institution. This report can be used to identify the primary reasons for any shift in the applicant population from the development sample. Bank management should generate a report for each characteristic and review them individually and as a total.

Final score report B This report measures the approval rate which results at the cutoff score and adherence to the scorecard. It shows applicants at each score level, and number of accepts and rejects. The report can also be used to analyze the effect of factors outside the scorecard.

Delinquency distributions report B This report monitors portfolio quality by score ranges. Two types of reports may be used. One measures how well a scorecard is working and the other measures current portfolio quality and changes in portfolio quality. The report compares accounts entering the portfolio at different times at equal stages in their account lives and reveals changes in the portfolio's behavior. Management should be identifying the causes for those changes. A vintage analysis table, which identifies accounts by year of origin, is used to compare a series of delinquency distributions reports and can be used to identify portfolio trends.

Portfolio chronology log B This log is an ongoing record of significant internal or external events used to record changes or events which could effect the performance of the accounts. The log helps explain causes of behavior in various tracking reports. Some examples of events that should be recorded are new marketing programs, application form changes, new override policies, new collection strategies, changes in the debt/income ratio, or income requirements.

Lender's override report B This type of report could identify volume of high- side and low-side overrides by month and year-to-date, provide a comparison over time and against the bank's benchmark, and could include reasons for the override.

Credit Card Allowance Methodology

Many banks use migration analyses to predict losses for the credit card portfolio. This technique is readily adaptable to the credit card environment and, when used on a rolling basis, provides a reasonable basis for estimating inherent loss in the portfolio. Most allowance for loan loss (ALL) models contemplate a level of adequacy based on extrapolating historical performance to the present portfolio. Initially, this can be estimated by applying the recent average loss experience to the present outstandings. Most often, the process involves varying degrees of portfolio segmentation in an effort to isolate significant portfolio segments which may be performing differently than the average.

Segmentation is useful in portfolio analysis, especially during periods of rapid expansion of new accounts booked through aggressive solicitations and acquisitions. Tracking these segments is a reasonable way to quantify the effect of changes in underwriting standards, economic conditions, management, and other factors outlined in the Comptroller's booklet titled *Allowance for Loan and Lease Losses*. Experience has shown that credit card portfolios will mirror the economic environment in which they operate. In fact, the unemployment rate typically demonstrates a strong correlation to the bank's credit card loss rate; when available, such data can be used to analyze specific portfolio segments.

Portfolio segmentation usually considers some aspect of portfolio delinquency, and generally divides the portfolio into various degrees of delinquency, or buckets, such as: 0-29 days, current; 30-59 days past due; 60-89 days past due, etc. Once segmented into various delinquency buckets, the degree of migration from one bucket to the next is measured over time; i.e., the bank's ALL model tracks the volume of loans which roll from, say, the 30-day bucket to the 60-day bucket, and measures this volume through a roll rate. Typically, as accounts age, the roll rate increases significantly. Application of the roll rates to the volume of loans in each bucket, including the current bucket, will provide some estimate of losses in the existing portfolio.
To illustrate: assume that the bank has tracked portfolio performance over the past several months and that, on average, 10 percent of the accounts in the current bucket in any given month, rolled (moved) to the 1-29 days past due bucket in the next month. Similarly, 25 percent of the accounts in the 1-29 day bucket rolled to the 30-day bucket in the next month; 50 percent of the accounts in the 30-day bucket rolled to the 60-day bucket, and so on. The bank could track the monthly performance over time and develop a data base for its model. The model might consider the roll rates for the most recent month; the most recent quarter; an average of several months or several quarters; an average over an infinite time horizon; an average employing a smoothing technique to emphasize more recent experience, and so on. Generally, the process improves as the historical data base and sophistication of the model increase.

In some cases, it may be appropriate to segment the portfolio into a variety of other components, particularly if other significant portfolio segments demonstrate materially different loss characteristics. Banks that offer a diversified credit card product base could analyze the allowance needs for each major product or program segment separately, such as Visa/MasterCard Gold versus Visa/MasterCard Classic, affinity cards, corporate and private label programs, and purchased portfolios. Similarly, portfolios may be segmented by vintage, or year of origin; by solicitation, or roll out; and by geography. Within each segment, the delinquency roll rates could be determined and applied to the outstandings within each bucket of that segment.

Most banks have mechanisms for dealing with delinquency exceptions. Some provisions can be made for an individual customer's unique circumstances through various special payment programs. These programs and other procedures can result in either a delay in the aging process, or a reaging of certain loans from a delinquent status to a current status. Since reaging affects the usual migration toward automatic charge off, examiners should assure themselves that the volumes involved in reaging, or any exceptional treatment, do not materially affect the delinquency rate or the automatic charge off and thus the reserve adequacy.

The examiner should determine that deferred aging or reaged volumes are not material. Most loans should routinely proceed through the aging and charge-off process without undue manipulation. If this is the case, it is likely that no further segmentation of reaged or special payment accounts is necessary in the analysis of ALLL adequacy.

Some credit card operations purify losses before charging them to the allowance. Capitalized interest and fees are reversed against appropriate income accounts, with principal only taken against the allowance. The examiner should determine whether losses are purified when analyzing the loss performance of the credit card department.

Profit Analysis

This is an example of a typical card issuer's income and expense statement. It may be used to monitor the earnings performance of the operation.

Total Portfolio Income and Expense Components
(Managed Assets Basis)

Category	First Period Income	Percent of Average Receivables	Second Period Income	Percent of Average Receivables	Third Period Income	Percent of Average Receivables
Interest Income						
Annual membership fees Late fees Overlimit fees Cash advance fees Other fees						
Cost of funds						
Net Interest Margin						
Loan losses Credit Bankruptcy Deceased Recoveries Net losses (excl. fraud) Net provision						
Non-interest income Interchange Other income Less rebates Net non-interest income						
Non-interest expense Account acquisition and credit processing Overlimit/collections Servicing/promotion Card holder billing Fraud investigation Processing interchange Processing payments Card issuing Authorizations Card administration **Outside services** Processing Fraud Misc. Expenses Total NIE						
Pre-tax income before allocations expenses						
Corporate allocation						
Net pre-tax income						

This is an example of a tracking shell used to monitor the performance of individual card programs.

Performance of Individual Portfolios
(Managed Assets Basis)

Portfolio	Pre-Tax Net Income First Period	Percent of Average Receivables	Average Receivables First Period	Average Receivables Second Period	Percent of Average Receivables	Pre-Tax Net Income Second Period
Classic						
Gold						
Affinity 1						
Affinity 2						
Affinity 3						
Affinity 4						
Affinity 5						
Cobrand 1						
Cobrand 2						
Cobrand 3						
Secured card						
Business card						
Other						
Total						

Note: The total pre-tax net income for periods 1 and 2 should agree with the net pre-tax net income reported in the gross portfolio income and expense components shell if these typical income statements are used together.

Impact of an Introductory Teaser Rate on Income

Finance charge income (pricing) is a key determinant of the profitability of a credit card operation. In recent years, competition for account holder growth has resulted in numerous marketing schemes involving introductory or teaser annual percentage rates (APRs), which ultimately affect finance charge revenues. Although the net effect of such marketing techniques to the income statement is not yet fully known, lowering APRs has a significant effect on profitability. For example, reducing the APR by 10 percent can result in a material decrease in the net margin, if all other factors remain constant.

The following example demonstrates the significant impact pricing strategies can have on an issuer's financial statement. A 10 percent price reduction results in a 47 percent compression of the net margin (4.3 percent to 2.3 percent). Even if the price reduction results in a 25 percent decrease in credit losses (3 percent to 2.25 percent), the net margin would still be 28 percent less than the original pricing strategy (4.3 percent to 3.05 percent). As a result, unless a bank adjusts the price for higher risk customers, decreasing the price (APR) for low-risk customers or to obtain new customers will dramatically impact net profit margins.

Sample Income Statement

	Original Rate	Reduction	10 and 25 Percent Price Reduction (Cost of Funds)
Finance charge	19.8	17.8 (-10)	17.8 (-10)
Cost of funds	(7.0)	(7.0)	(7.0)
Net interest margin	12.8	10.8 (-16)	10.80 (-16)
Fee income	1.0	1.0	1.00
Charge-offs	(3.0)	(3.0)	(2.25) (-25)
Non-interest expense	(6.5)	(6.5)	(6.50)
Net margin	4.3	2.3 (-47)	3.05 (-28)

Types of Users

The ratio of convenience users (accounts of customers who accrue no finance charges because they pay in full each billing cycle) to revolvers (those who make less than full payments) plays a significant role in finance charge revenue. The greater the percentage of convenience users in the portfolio, the lower the yield produced by the portfolio. Also, the bank must fund the convenience users' receivables while in many instances only benefiting from incoming interchange revenues. Depending upon the product, it may take $5 million to $10 million in purchase sales volume per account to produce enough incoming interchange revenue just to break even on a convenience user account.

Purchased Credit Card Relationships

As of first quarter 1993, banks were permitted to include purchased credit card relationships (PCCRs) in regulatory capital computations. To qualify, management must perform quarterly impairment tests on the PCCRs. The failure of management to accurately perform these tests could render the PCCRs ineligible for inclusion in regulatory capital computations. To properly conduct a review of PCCRs for impairment and inclusion into regulatory capital computations, the examiner will need to review (for each portfolio that has a booked PCCR) the original acquisition model, the most recent discounted cash flow and fair market value models, and related data to support drivers and assumptions.

FFIEC Instructions for the Reports of Condition and Income require banks with PCCRs to perform a quarterly impairment test to ensure the intangible is adequately supported by the estimated future net cash flows from the acquired portfolio. An impaired PCCR means that the discounted amount of future net cash flows is below the book carrying value of the PCCR, thus requiring a write down. Management must, at a minimum, perform the following to comply with FFIEC instructions:

1. Management must determine the inherent discount rate used in the acquisition of the portfolio. Because there are numerous methods management may have used to determine the purchase price of the portfolio, the OCC has established a common method to determine the inherent discount rate. The inherent discount rate is "based upon the *estimated future net cash flows and the price paid at the time of purchase*" (Banking Bulletin 93-16). Accordingly, to determine the inherent discount rate used in a portfolio purchase, the estimated future net cash flows of the portfolio are discounted at a rate that produces a net present value equal to the premium paid for the portfolio. These should be true cash flows, without non-cash items included. If 10 percent of the portfolio is funded by equity capital in the acquisition model, similar leverage in the valuation model described in step 2 below should result. Typically, these models run 10 years or less in estimated cash flows. On affinity and/or private label portfolios that contain specific contract maturities (e.g., 3, 5, or 7 years), the models should generally not exceed the contract maturity. The determination of the inherent discount rate must be performed for each portfolio for which there is a PCCR. The failure to accurately perform this step may result in a PCCR being declared ineligible for inclusion in regulatory capital computations.

2. Management must value the portfolio, on a quarterly basis, using a discount rate not less than the original discount rate inherent in the asset acquisition. Furthermore, a discounted cash flow model is required to be used in the valuation. Using this valuation technique, the book value of the PCCR must not exceed the discounted amount of estimated future net cash flows. Management is currently permitted to use a pool-by-pool or an aggregate method to determine impairment. If, on an aggregate basis, impairment appears to exist, discuss with the EIC and management before requesting any write down. This step must be performed for each portfolio for which there is a PCCR. The failure to accurately perform this step may result in a PCCR being declared ineligible for inclusion in regulatory capital computations.

Typically, management uses a model which reduces the years of remaining cash flows periods as each quarter passes. For example, if management started with a 10-year model and six months have passed since the purchase, the valuation model would have nine and one-half years of cash flows remaining. In each model, management generally includes a termination value for the receivables remaining after the cash flow periods have been exhausted to simulate a portfolio sale. These termination values usually run between 10 percent and 25 percent, reflecting the premiums which are currently being realized in today's marketplace for credit card portfolios. If the termination values exceed this range, management should provide support for the value chosen.

The assumptions used for these valuations should be reflective of recent trends of the portfolio. Many banks use the previous year's results as the drivers for the current year's models. Any significant variance from past actual experience should be questioned.

3. For regulatory capital computations, the following rules must be followed:

a) Tier I capital for PCCRs is limited to 25 percent.

b) Management must determine the value of qualifying intangibles for capital purposes at the lesser of (a) 90 percent of fair value, or (b) 100 percent of unamortized book value.

Management subsequently must determine the current fair market value of each intangible asset included in Tier I capital at least quarterly. In doing so, management must "apply an appropriate market discount rate to the expected net cash flows of the intangible asset." In essence, the discount rate used in step 2 is replaced with a market discount rate.

4. The OCC's *Bank Accounting Advisory Series* (BAAS) states that PCCRs "should be amortized over their estimated useful lives, not to exceed 10 years." Also, BAAS requires national banks to use an accelerated amortization method, because such methods generally provide for periodic amortization that best corresponds to the benefit expected from the asset. The straight-line method, however, may be used when the resulting amortization approximates the amount that would be recorded under an accelerated method. Many banks do not comply with this requirement and use a straight-line amortization method because it reduces the earnings impact in the early years. The amortization schedules for each PCCR should be reviewed to ensure appropriateness as well as compliance with OCC guidelines. Preferably, the amortization schedule should approximate the revenue stream generated by the portfolio; i.e., if 20 percent of the revenue is being recognized in the first year, it would be prudent to amortize 20 percent of the PCCR in that time frame.

There are numerous methods of performing valuations, some relatively aggressive and some conservative. For example, the valuation model may not include a termination value which could significantly increase the projected worth of the card portfolio and therefore support the booked PCCR.

When portfolios are acquired, many banks set up an allowance for possible booked loan losses for the portfolio the same time the receivables are acquired. In setting up the ALLL, many banks capitalize the ALLL provision expense and amortize it over future periods, not to exceed 10 years. The BAAS limits capitalization of the provision expense to situations in which management has documented the ALLL that was on the seller's books at the time of acquisition. Moreover, the capitalized portion may not exceed what was on the seller's books. Any portion in excess must be added to current expenses when the assets are booked.

Example of Components in a Valuation Model

The following components often will be disclosed or projected in a typical acquisition/valuation model for actual and projected periods:

Total receivables   Average receivables

Amortization period (years)
Percent of receivables capital   funded
Percent of premium capital funded
Accounts:
    current
    acquisitions
    attrition rate
    percent variable
Revenue:
    finance charge
    interchange
    cash advance fee
    annual fee
    overlimit fee
    late fee
Total fees
Total revenue
Funding:
    portfolio cost of funds
    funding of unamortized
    premium   credits

Discount rate
Discount value
Return on assets
Return on equity

Net cost of funds
 Losses:
    charge-offs
    recoveries
Net charge-offs
Operating expenses:
    recovery expense
    collection expense
    credit expense
    customer service expense
    development expense Operations expense:
    systems expense
    processing expense
    conversion expense
    other
Total operating expense
Termination value
Federal income tax
Net income

Sample Request Letter

Bank name
Bank charter number
Examination date

Please provide the following information as of the close of business *xxxxxx* unless otherwise noted. Also, please provide lists of codes and definitions, where applicable, for each requested report.

General

1)   Organization charts for the credit card division, including each major functional area, and brief resumes for all principal positions.

2)   A list of board and executive management committees that supervise the credit card operation, including a list of members and meeting schedules. Also, copies of minutes documenting those meetings since the last examination and the most current board information packet.

3)   Copies of management compensation programs, including any incentive plans.

4)   The latest management information reports supplied to the head of your credit card operation on a monthly basis.

5)   A report summarizing the number of accounts and dollars outstanding for each status code.

6)   Actual-to-plan comparison reports for *xxxx* and year-to-date *xxxx*.

7)   A balance sheet and income statement as of *xxxx*.

8)   Copies of the *xxxx* and *xxxx* budget, including any budget revisions year-to-date *xxxx*.

9)   Copies of the division's business and/or strategic plan including any long-range projections.

10)   Copies of any internal and external audit reports (including compliance), with management responses, conducted for the credit card division during the last year.

11)   Copies of any loan review or consultant reports conducted for the credit card division during the last year.

12)   A list of all outside vendors used by the division, the services rendered by each, and a list of most recent audit reports available for those vendors, copies of contracts, customer service contacts with phone numbers, and vendor financial statements.

13)   Copies of terms and conditions for each program with recourse arrangements with agent banks, private label clients, etc., if applicable.

14) A list of credit card securitizations and copies of the prospectus associated with those offerings.

15) Copies of Visa, MasterCard, or other applicable association standards. Also, copies of correspondence received from the bankcard organizations within the past year.

Credit Underwriting

16) A copy of your policies and procedures for credit underwriting.

17) A copy of each scorecard used and a description of its age (when developed), the vendor, and which portfolio it is used for. Also, for each scorecard please provide the associated:

- Odds table;
- Scorecard override reports; and
- Summary report detailing accounts segregated by score range.

18) A list of approval rates by type (take-ones, cross-selling/branch, telemarketing, direct mail solicitation, preapproved direct mail solicitation, other, and overall approval rate).

19) A list of credit limits granted for each card program:

- Maximum;
- Minimum; and
- Most common.

20) A description of behavior scoring models, if used, identifying which functions applied to (e.g., account approval, portfolio maintenance, line increases, etc.). In addition, please provide the associated:

- Odds table;
- Scorecard override reports; and
- Summary of portfolio by score range.

21) Copies of reports on card holder account statistics that detail information such as:

- Total number of accounts on file;
- Total number of accounts with balances;
- Percentage of accounts with revolving balances;
- Total cards issued;
- Total credit committed;
- Outstanding balances;
- Average account balances; and
- Average credit line on file.

22) A print screen copy of the application processing system screens, with necessary field definitions and codes.

23) If you use direct mail or telemarketing programs, a copy of the criteria used to generate solicitation lists.

24) A copy of the terms/criteria for "skip-a-payment" programs, if applicable.

25) A copy of the terms/criteria for "pay-ahead" features, if used. Do these or other programs accrue finance charges on capitalized interest?

Marketing

26) A list of the number of card accounts acquired in *xxxx*, *xxxx*, and year-to-date *xxxx*, by product.

27) A report showing the percentage of card accounts acquired by source (e.g., portfolio acquisition, direct mail solicitation, take-one, standard/classic upgrade, cross-selling, other) for *xxxx*, *xxxx*, and year-to-date *xxxx*.

28) A list of attrition rates for *xxxx*, *xxxx*, and year-to-date *xxxx*, overall and by product. If possible, please differentiate between bank- and customer-initiated closure.

29) A copy of a product manual which details all card programs outstanding and their contractual terms.

30) A list of marketing costs for *xxxx*, *xxxx*, and year-to-date *xxxx*, with detail showing:

- Marketing cost per new account, by product; and
- Marketing cost per active account, by product.

31) A summary report detailing the number of accounts and dollars outstanding for accounts at zero interest rates and rates below contractual/market terms.

Collections

32) A copy of policy and procedure manuals for collections including:

- Reaging;
- Fixed payment or cure programs;
- Settlements;
- Forgiveness programs; and
- Overline accounts.

Also, please include charge-off policies for credit losses, bankruptcies, fraud, and deceased accounts.

33) A summary report of contractual delinquencies for the total portfolio and for each program.

34) A summary report of charge-off ratios for the total portfolio and for each program.

35) A description of how delinquent accounts are assigned to collectors.

36) A copy of your reaged accounts report, both cumulative and for the last 12 months.

37) A copy of your fixed payment report (Consumer Credit Counseling Service accounts and other programs where payments are fixed).

38) A copy of the collection matrix which details the collection strategies currently in use.

39)   A print screen copy of the collection system screens, with necessary field definitions and codes.

Risk Management

40)   Copies of reports produced by risk management on a regular basis.

Fraud

41)   A copy of the policies and procedures for the fraud area.

42)   A description of methods used to determine fraudulent activities.

43)   A summary report on accounts block coded fraud.

Due Diligence/Portfolio Acquisition

44)   A copy of the procedures used to perform due diligence for potential portfolio acquisitions.

45)   A description of the process used to evaluate the results of due diligence reviews, incorporation of that information into an acquisition pricing model(s), and the personnel involved.

46)   A list of portfolios acquired since *xxxx*.

Management Information Systems

47)   A copy of the written policy or other guidelines for management information system requirements.

48)   A narrative and diagram of the work flow for the roll up of information, modification/entry points, and the controls within those points.

49)   A written description and flow chart for transaction work flow from source through settlement.

50)   A list of all hardware, software, and all networks that feed management information systems.

51)   The contingency plans for the bank/department.

52)   The policies and procedures for reviewing vendor financial statements.

53)   A copy of the strategic projects development plan as it relates to MIS projects. Please include the following information and copies of examples where appropriate:

- Project objectives and time frames;
- Describe project management method used; and
- Describe methods used to monitor project performance.

Allowance for Loan and Lease Losses

54)   Allowance for loan and lease loss methodology and most recent analysis.

Commission or Gift for Procuring a Loan	
Laws	18 USC 215
Equal Credit Opportunity Act	
Laws	15 USC 1691 *et seq.*
Regulations	12 CFR 202
Fair Credit Reporting Act	
Laws	15 USC 1681 *et seq.*
Fair Debt Collection Practices Act	
Laws	15 USC 1692
Financial Institution Records	
Regulations	31 CFR 103.33
Legal Lending Limit	
Laws	12 USC 84
Regulations	12 CFR 32
Loans to Affiliates	
Laws	12 USC 371c
Loans to Insiders	
Laws	12 USC 375a, 375b
Regulations	12 CFR 215
Political Contributions and Loans	
Laws	2 USC 431 (8)(a); 2 USC 441b
Statutory Bad Debts	
Laws	12 USC 56
Tie-in Provisions	
Laws	12 USC 1971 *et seq.*
Truth in Lending Act	
Laws	15 USC 1601 *et seq.*
Regulations	12 CFR 226